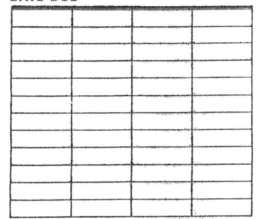

D1597650

THE
WORLD'S
EYE

THE
WORLD'S
EYE

Albert M. Potts

THE UNIVERSITY PRESS OF KENTUCKY

For Esther

Library of Congress Cataloging in Publication Data

Potts, Albert M.
  The world's eye.

  Includes bibliographical references and index.
  1. Eye—Mythology. 2. Eye—Folklore. 3. Eye—
Miscellanea. I. Title.
BL325.E93P67   398'.353   79-4009
ISBN 0-8131-1387-3   AACR2

Scholarly publisher for the Commonwealth,
serving Berea College, Centre College of Kentucky,
Eastern Kentucky University, The Filson Club,
Georgetown College, Kentucky Historical Society,
Kentucky State University, Morehead State University,
Murray State University, Northern Kentucky University,
Transylvania University, University of Kentucky,
University of Louisville, and Western Kentucky University.

Editorial and Sales Offices: Lexington, Kentucky 40506-0024

Contents

List of Illustrations

Acknowledgments

First and foremost I must acknowledge the contribution of Mrs. Edith G. Rawraway Goldman, my longtime associate and friend. She gave help in every aspect of the work, from obtaining hard-to-get references to typing several of the preliminary drafts of the manuscript. This book could not have appeared without her assistance.

The cooperation and kindness of the staff of the University Press of Kentucky is acknowledged with pleasure.

A host of individuals over the years have made contributions to my information on one or more of the subject areas treated in the book or have added to my collection of amulets. If the name of any of these generous people has been omitted, it is through oversight, not by intent. They are: Mrs. Ursula v. Berlepsch, Dr. Genevieve Miller, Professor and Mrs. Isaac Michaelson, Dr. Ilza Veith, the late Dr. Maxwell Gittelsohn, Dr. and Mrs. John Pataki, Professor Frank W. Newell, Professor Alfred Bühler, Professor Gerhard Lindblom, Professor Stephan Beyer, Leon and Polly Miller, Dr. Evan Mauer, Ira and Janina Marks, Professor Fernando Camara, Professor Gordon F. Ekholm, Dr. Phillip H. Lewis, the late Munro Leaf, Dame Kathleen Kenyon, Mrs. Helen Cooperman, Mr. Alan R. Sawyer, Mr. David L. DeJarnette, Mrs. Chira Chongkol, Professor Christian Kaufmann, and Professor H. J. Wehrli.

Credit lines with the individual illustrations identify the many institutions and individuals who have granted me permission to use photographs of objects in their possession. Where no other attribution appears, the object is in the author's own collection.

1. Introduction

That vision is by far the most important of the senses few will debate. That the eye is the seat of vision any primitive or two-year-old can determine with certainty by covering the eyes. Add to this that the eyes are the center of expressiveness, the windows of the soul, and it is easy to understand what a potent and universal symbol the eye has been since earliest prehistory.[1] It is the object of this book to consider how wonder and the primitive mentality (in the absence of true scientific knowledge) have endowed the eye with special properties, and to seek out what special significance the eye possesses as a symbol.

This then is not a book about the exactly described and precisely defined eye of the ophthalmic scientist. It is about how all the world exclusive of scientists looks upon the eye. It is about the World's Eye.

On such a quest there are three principal directions for exploration. First, prehistoric artifacts and the records of ancient civilizations furnish us with the ideas of a less sophisticated time. Second, the folklore of our own times—both that of primitive tribes and that of the peasantry—serves as an additional storehouse of information. Finally, it has been suggested by numerous psychiatrists—principally those of the Jungian school—that by a type of psychological recapitulation the unconscious minds of all of us partake of the most primitive mental mechanisms.[2] Thus the aspects of the unconscious exposed by mental disease give us a third window on the symbolism of the eye.

As an intruder from the biological sciences into this territory that lies somewhere between psychology and anthropology, I feel it necessary to state some ground rules for the material that follows. Although they may be standard for the social sciences, as a newcomer I must spell them out to make sure there are no misapprehensions by me or by the reader.

My material treats of primitive basic thought processes in the mind of man, but when one goes to the primitive societies that are the origin of some of the material there are multiple barriers to truly definitive understanding of what the material means. The thing that would most nearly approximate scientific proof of a hypothesis would be for several reliable anthropologists studying primitive tribes in widely separated areas to have come up with identical answers to the questions I pose and in addition for the same view to be confirmed by one or more writers in antiquity.

Needless to say this kind of verification never occurs.

For one thing, the anthropologists have rarely asked the particular questions we want answered. When they do ask such questions, they are often answered by silence or deception, or they get multiple and conflicting answers, or they get the honest admission that the tribe no longer knows the reason for doing something in a particular way.[3] A curious modern commentary on purposeful deception is the treatment in southern Italy of the stranger who wants to discuss the question of amulets against the Evil Eye. A shopkeeper may have a dozen such amulets on display, but if the word "malocchio" (Evil Eye) is mentioned the stranger is diverted to something else, or the shopkeeper disappears. The word to use is "portafortuna" (lucky piece). This may be mentioned without breaching the code and a purchase may be made.

As another obstacle to obtaining clear explanations, motives for doing anything, even in a primitive society, are rarely single and direct. The headhunters along the Sepik River in New Guinea (Melanesians) and the Maori of New Zealand (Polynesians) preserved the heads both of ancestors and of enemies conquered in battle.[4] The differences in the treatment of these two classes of heads and in the attitudes of the tribesmen toward them are not clearly defined. Thus, even if one could do one's own field work and if there were enough cooperative and reliable informants in surviving primitive tribes, the finds would be suspect; the one sure way to invalidate results would be to ask questions with a particular objective. It would be all too easy to get the answers one was looking for.

Even less help can be expected from the ancients. Most seriously, large parts of the record are missing. There is no text material that connects the iconography of the Mesopotamian cylinder seals with the written record. The Shang bronzes of ancient China appear in a historical void where there is no written record at all, and the snatches of inscription on late Shang and Chou pieces contribute nothing to our knowledge of their motifs. The little that is written about the Gorgon is late and is already fitted by Hesiod into the mold of classical Greek mythology. Any hint of origins is lost.

Thus, not only is there little documentation for answers to our questions, but there is not the slightest hope that more anthropological expeditions, more ar-

Figure 1. Eye idols. Figurines excavated at Tel Brak by Sir M. E. L. Mallowan. Reproduced by permission of Prof. Mallowan.

cheological investigations, or another hundred clay tablets published will bring us any nearer to a believable answer.

In those categories all that is left is the body of artifacts from antiquity and from anthropological investigation. Add to these the contributions of psychiatry and of modern folklore. The uses that I make of these factors and the juxtapositions are purely my own. They are colored by my position in the relatively unromantic twentieth century and by personal biases which I am in no position to analyze. My request is just that the reader look at these syntheses through my eyes for a moment and ask himself whether they may not seem valid to him too.

It is certain that the miracle of vision has been as fundamental to man through the ages as it seems to us now. One need not belabor the survival value of keen vision nor the fact that the disaster of blindness is even greater in a primitive culture than it is in ours. Let me cite a single instance where isolated artifacts unsupported by other material tell an eloquent and irrefutable story.

In the excavation of Tel Brak, a site in the Khabur Valley of eastern Syria, M. E. L. Mallowan uncovered a temple which he named the Eye Temple. The name came, logically enough, from the thousands of alabaster figurines found there in which the eyes were the completely dominant feature (Fig. 1). The level at which these figurines were found was dated by Mallowan at 3,000 B.C.—the very dawn of civilization. This was the protohistoric period in Mesopotamia, the Jemdat-Nasr period, when writing had just begun. It was contemporary with the First Dynasty of Egypt and the earliest Minoan culture on Crete. The find of eye figurines has prompted numerous speculations on their nature and purpose, and the predictable debate about whether they were amulets or symbols or idols has arisen.[5] In cold reality we have nothing more than the find itself and its geographical and chronological location. For our purposes there is no need to construct from this, as O. G. S. Crawford has done, a fertility cult worshiping an eye-goddess form of Ishtar and extending through the entire Mediterranean into the Atlantic as far up the coast as Ireland.[6] But the very existence of the Tel Brak figurines is a concrete expression of a primitive society's wonder at vision and the eye.

Crawford's speculation about the Eye Goddess does bring up a subject beset with booby traps and polemics—the subject of cultural diffusion. In some of the subject areas treated below—the Evil Eye, the Ojo de Dios, the Apotropaic Eye—really identical concepts or artifacts or both are found half a world apart. It is tempting to speculate about whether these arose independently or spread from a single source. I suppose everyone must form a private opinion on the subject sooner or later and vigorous advocacy of some position is easy. However, it is the duty of the laboratory scientist venturing onto this unfirm ground to bring the expedition up short. With only the artifacts in hand, the thesis for (or against) would evoke controversy that would distract unduly from the job at hand. Fortunately, for our needs there is no necessity to solve the riddle of cultural diffusion, but the areas where the question arises will be pointed out in passing.

Let there be no doubt, however, that the central theme of what follows—the Ariadne thread through the maze of ancient objects and modern ideas—is that of the eye and vision. Use will be made of anthropology or iconography or art history or psychiatry where these are appropriate. Indeed, some ideas from each of those fields may be found juxtaposed in new and possibly useful ways. However, this is a book about the eye, and patterns of symbolism associated with it, not one about anthropology or psychiatry.

In the material to follow, a logical beginning is the Evil Eye. The Evil Eye notion is so powerful that it truly antedates all historical records and is still alive today. The center of the belief lies, at least today, in the Mediterranean basin. If one needed to emphasize the liveliness of the Evil Eye idea there is a 1977 novel called *Minnie Santangelo and the Evil Eye*, set in New York's Little Italy and using much of the material discussed in the next and subsequent chapters.[7]

Another treatment of the topic can be seen in a 1976 book, *The Evil Eye*, written by anthropologists and from a narrowly anthropological point of view.[8] It is as far from my goal as one can get. The multiple authorship necessarily makes for a lack of homogeneity in depth of treatment. To my mind the ancient aspects and folklore dealt with in the early chapters are treated superficially. A later chapter, couched in the jargon of the social sciences, uses multifactorial mathematical analysis to lend authority to material that is to me patent nonsense. Most to the point, the *eye* part of the

Evil Eye gets scant attention in those pages. This is a perfect example of what is not being attempted here.

A natural complement to the subject of the Evil Eye is the subject of amulets that protect against it. Once again, the notion of "amulet" is psychologically a complex one. Some of the complexities are documented by Petrie in his book on the topic. Petrie cites five "more obvious" ideas which underlie the use of amulets. These are enumerated below.

(A) The psychic effect of giving confidence and self-reliance, and the intent to live; with the result that the wearer would thus be fortified to steer through dangers without faltering, or would be saved from that terrible weakening due to fear, which often kills men as surely as knife or poison kills. To possess a charm which would defy *tabu* would be a vast advantage in lower forms of culture.

(B) The direction of thought to any physical weakness or disease, may have a very beneficial effect on illness; and the possession of an amulet supposed to benefit the patient may easily act as a faith-healer and promote real recovery.

(C) The idea of a double or *alter ego* of different organs, connected with them in a mystic way, may be a purpose of amulets. In the tale of Anpu and Bata, the heart of Bata is set in a tree, and anything that happens to it happens also to him. So it might be imagined that a kidney-stone, a blood-stone, an eye-stone, or various other objects supposed to be connected with different organs, would by the care and attention paid to them have a reflex action in strengthening the organ involved.

(D) The provision of a vicarious double, to which evils and diseases may be transferred from the body. An object resembling the disease, or a model of the organ, might be supposed to receive the attacks of the malignant spirits to whom diseases are usually credited, and so save the real person.

(E) The influence often called "sympathetic magic" which might perhaps best be named "the doctrine of similars." Objects which have a similarity one to another, are supposed to be necessarily connected; they are in touch with the abstract quality or influence which has to be evoked: They generally act by producing a similarity in the person, but otherwise by averting a similarity, on the plea that the event has already taken place, and cannot therefore happen again.[9]

It is clear that no single one of the ideas is operative in the use of amulets against the Evil Eye. Each plays a role that varies with circumstances.

Of the amulets against the Evil Eye (and against other forms of nameless ill fortune, to be sure) amulets in the shape of an eye demand special attention. They partake of the fourth and fifth qualities listed by

Figure 2. "Watchbird." Drawing by Munro Leaf. Reproduced by permission of Mr. Leaf.

Petrie. Of all eye amulets the Eye of Horus deserves and gets prime consideration. It is one of the oldest and longest-lived amulets. It may, since it comes from ancient Egypt, be one of the very earliest signs we have available of the existence of the evil eye-amulet duo. These matters are treated in chapter 3.

A somewhat different group of ideas still concerned with how we think about the eye and vision has been described by me in a previous essay as "the Watchbird Concept Complex."[10] The "Watchbird" drawings of the children's artist Munro Leaf seemed to me to typify this cluster of ideas (see, for example, the drawing in Fig. 2). The first idea of this cluster is that one's actions are being watched constantly. Long before Munro Leaf, a primitive tribe in a remote part of Mexico incorporated this into a religious concept and created an amuletic object that embodies this basic idea about seeing. That idea is expanded in chapter 7, "The Ojo de Dios."

An expansion of this notion is that divine surveillance does not merely monitor conduct but that it is benevolent in nature. This is the concept behind the eye-in-triangle symbol whose history has not been carefully documented before. That fascinating story which runs from Greek antiquity to the Founding Fathers of the United States is told in chapter 8, "The Eye of Providence."

Not implicit in the Watchbird concept itself but a logical extension of the idea is that the watcher can protect the watched and turn away evil from him by the watcher's horrible and repellent appearance. This notion, too, is embedded in the mind of men. It is shared by the ancients and by primitive tribes and has been appropriately named "The Apotropaic Eye." The incorporation of this notion into symbols is described in chapter 4, "The Eye of Medusa," titled after one of the potent symbols. The connection between the Apotropaic Eye and some primitive masks is quite real to me and appears in chapter 5, "Behind the Mask."

The extra force of large numbers is implicit in much primitive symbolism. How this occurs in relation to the eye is shown in chapter 6, "The Eyes of Argus."

There are many more aspects of the topic on which I have not touched for various reasons—some because they seem too fanciful, others because one must stop researching at some point and begin writing if a book is ever to result. That the research could go on for many more years is the final tribute to the ubiquity, the all-pervasiveness, and the vital importance of eye symbolism in the mind of man.

2. The Evil Eye

As Wallis Budge said so well, early man lived "days of misery and nights of fear." The forces against his staying alive were so numerous and so potent that he personified them as devils, demons, and evil spirits.[1] There is every reason to believe that the concept of the Evil Eye went right along with the demons, for amulets are among the finds in prehistoric archeological sites and the Evil Eye concept is found in historical times in all cultures and in every part of the globe.

It was once fashionable to ask about such universal concepts (of which the biblical legend of the flood is one) whether they had sprung up independently or whether they emanated from a single source. We have finally begun to realize that while such questions are now answerable in the precise sense, they are also to a large extent meaningless. Best evidence has it that man as we know him, *Homo sapiens*, with our stature and our brain capacity, has existed on earth for some forty thousand years.[2] It is possible to place some human intellectual concepts with more or less accuracy in the three thousand years of recorded history. The legal concepts of Hammurabi, the Socratic method, the idea of the circulation of the blood are some of these. Many other ideas are so obviously part of the human condition, so intimately linked with birth, death, and the necessities of being alive that they belong to the ten-times-longer period of prehistory. They are still with us in the historical period because those necessities are still with us, but they begin with man, not with any written record. The concept of the Evil Eye was one of those ideas.

In this frame of reference it is easy to understand the idea that a malign influence working at a distance can cause harm. The result may be loss of crops, loss of domestic animals, even loss of life itself. That the influence is thought to be transmitted by a glance is also easily understandable, for the ability of the countenance to convey feelings of hatred (or affection) needs no elaboration. The selection of the eye as the actual transmission agent for harm is not surprising in view of the mysterious power of seeing for the primitive subject and in view of the role the eyes play in facial expression. The oldest written reference occurs in Sumerian cuneiform texts which describe how the great god Ea went forth against the Evil Eye.[3] Ancient Hebrew designates the Evil Eye by r'a ayin and in the

Book of Proverbs one reads "Eat thou not the bread of him that hath an evil eye" (Prov. 23:6). Similarly there is an Egyptian hieroglyph given by Budge as equivalent to the Evil Eye, and an account of spells on the wall of the temple of Edfu intended to accomplish the Eye's destruction.[4] The concept is found in Siam and Malaya, in Sumatra and Tahiti, in Greenland and Alaska, in Nicaragua and Mexico, among the Bantu and the Australian bushmen.[5] Thus one is dealing with a truly universal idea.

Another token of the fundamental and universal nature of the Evil Eye is how deeply embedded it is in the language. Every language, ancient and modern, has its equivalent word. To list only a few there are:

German:	böse Blick	Danish:	et ondt öje
Italian:	malocchio	Syriac:	aina bîshâ
Spanish:	mal de ojo	Hungarian:	szemverés
French:	mauvais œil	Sanskrit:	ghoram caksuh

The Greek expression is *baskanos ophthalmos*, said by Delrio—a sixteenth-century Jesuit from Liege—to be of Chaldaic origin. The Latin *fascinatio* is a direct derivative of *baskanos* and our word *fascinate* originally had the same meaning. (Its present-day usage reflects the same sort of shift we see in *enchanting* and *bewitching*.) A word of similar meaning is the Latin *invidere*: to look closely upon, whence *invidia*: the Evil Eye (Cicero), and English *envy*.[6]

It is all the easier to appreciate the basic nature of the Evil Eye idea when we realize that the standard theory of vision among ancient authors held that the eye saw by *projecting* something on the object of regard. Pythagoras, Empedocles of Agrigentum, Plato, and Galen all subscribed to some form of this theory.[7] The idea was sufficiently alive in the popular mind in the mid-seventeenth century that Thomas Browne felt it necessary to set the record right in his *Pseudodoxia Epidemica*. Right along with this idea and juxtaposed to it in Browne's book is his account of the legendary basilisk or cockatrice. He says: "According to the doctrine of the ancients men still affirm that it killeth at a distance, that it poisoneth by the eye and by priority of vision." The basilisk is a member of Pliny's legendary menagerie. The Roman described the creature as a crested snake, king of all the serpents which progresses erect and not prone. The basilisk could wither shrubs, split rocks, and kill any human beholder at a glance. Browne deals with the problem in a not completely forthright way but concludes that the supporters of the basilisk must be mixed up just as were those who believed in the eye as a projector: "And therefore this conceit was probably begot by such as held the opinion of sight by extramission; as did *Pithagorus, Plato, Empedocles, Hipparchus, Galen, Macrobius, Proclus, Simplicius* with most of the Ancients and is the postulate of *Euclide* in his Opticks; but now sufficiently convicted from observations of the dark chamber." Of the sort of stories with which Browne had to contend, typical is this encounter with a basilisk in Vienna in June 1212, still being described in 1858: a baker's apprentice who had gone to the well to draw water gazed upon a basilisk in the well and died the same day. The house where this occurred was still pointed out more than 600 years later.[8]

It was a naïve notion of the writer as an ophthalmologist, before realizing the deeply and exclusively psychological quality of the concept, that folklore must have assigned some distinguishing physical characteristics to the eye capable of causing evil. Actually the literature is notably sparse in physical descriptions of the persons who possess the Evil Eye, although the specifications that do exist are rewardingly curious. Adequate consideration shows that it is necessary from a practical viewpoint for the possessor to be inconspicuous—otherwise he could be avoided with ease and disaster could not be explained by this mechanism.

There are occasional statements that strabismic, one-eyed, exophthalmic, or enophthalmic individuals may be fascinators. In northern countries those with dark eyes, in Mediterranean countries the blue-eyed, have been similarly accused. More distinctive is the specification of differently colored irises.[9] (This may well mean trouble, but trouble for the possessor who may have heterochromic iridocyclitis.)

Probably the most intriguing of all, however, is the statement of Pliny, who, quoting from assorted Greek authors, describes the women of Scythia and of Pontus who can cause cattle to die, trees to wither, and babies to perish. These "have a double pupil in one eye and the image of a horse in the other." This is a strange set of properties, to say the least. A delightfully sensible explanation of the horse was made by Dalecamp, a sixteenth-century editor of Pliny (and rejected by Smith on poetic grounds).[10] The suggestion was that Pliny read the Greek *hippos* and translated it *effigiem equi*— "the image of a horse"—when the source meant to indicate the pathological entity hippus—either nystagmus or what we now call spontaneous widening and narrowing of the pupil. This is a version eminently acceptable to a physician. The double-pupil idea must have been a well-accepted piece of contemporary culture, for Ovid over fifty years earlier describing the witchery of his mistress (and incidentally voicing the emission theory of vision) says (*Amores* 1.8.15–16): "oculis quoque pupula duplex / fulminat et gemino lumen ab orbe venit." ("In her eyes, too, a double pupil shines, and a beam darts from her double orb.")

Let us rest assured, however, that the ordinary, garden-variety Evil Eye belonged to a person whose only peculiarity was his presence at the site of a series of misfortunes—witness the reputations of Pope Pius IX and King Alfonso XIII of Spain, who were famous as "jettatori" in southern Italy. The term *jettatore* itself, which is indigenous to southern Italy and Sicily, comes from the Latin *jactare* (to throw). The local term for fascinator once again derives from the projection theory of vision; and describes the ability of the unfortunate, and often unwilling, possessor of the Evil Eye to project his evil influence from his eyes.

The theme of the unwilling fascinator entered the fiction of the last century. As a twentieth-century writer is alert for any possibility that he can sell Hollywood a scenario, the nineteenth-century novelist frequently bore in mind the possibility that his book could provide the libretto for a grand opera. Théophile Gautier's *Jettatura*, for example, gets the full grand-opera treatment. The charming, vigorous English girl visiting Naples becomes attracted to the youthful but dark and moody Italian count. As their acquaintance progresses, the girl falls ill. Servants begin to avoid the count's visits, and finally they desert the villa of the English family. The family is the last to learn that the count, truly in love with the girl, is a *jettatore*. The girl dies, ostensibly of tuberculosis, and the count walks into the sea in an act of despair and expiation.

For another indicator of the common basic ideas about vision, one can go to psychiatric case reports and the literature of psychiatry. The psychiatric material divides itself into two separate categories. In one of these categories is evidence that sustains our thesis on the fundamental role that the eye and vision play in human thought processes. Indeed, so basic is the connection that loss of precious sight is the punishment for intolerable or forbidden conduct. In the other category is material which echoes the already quoted concepts of the Evil Eye and the projection theory of vision.

Examples of the first category are found in the writings of Karl Abraham and of Sigmund Freud. Abraham coined the term *scopophilia* (pleasure in looking) and described after Freud how this pleasure may be the subject of inner conflict. If the impulse is too strong or directed toward forbidden objects, serious emotional disturbances may occur. Freud's essay deals specifically with his experience with hysterical blindness. In his terminology this symptom is caused by ego-repression of the offending function according to a psychological *lex talionis*. He fortifies his interpretation by quoting the Godiva legend and the fact that blindness was the punishment for Peeping Tom.[11] He could have carried his point still farther by citing the legend of Santa Lucia of Syracuse. Her beautiful eyes attracted a young and noble lover. In consternation she plucked them out and sent them to the young man on a silver platter.[12]

In the second category—psychiatric reports directly pertinent to the Evil Eye—is the work of Phyllis Greenacre based on forty-one of her own cases. Her overall conclusion was that in the fantasy of the mentally ill the eye is not merely a sex symbol but the organ betraying the guilt of the soul. This, according to Dr. Greenacre, is a dramatization by the patient of an early belief that the demon of insanity who ordinarily secluded himself in the pelvis was now in possession of body and soul and was looking out through the eyes. Here not only are the eyes considered the windows of the soul but the malevolence of the glance creates a truly evil eye.[13]

Greenacre quotes the specific case of a woman brought into the Phipps Clinic after a suicide attempt. The patient had both eyes bandaged, for she thought that it would make others blind to see her eyes. Later, in the hospital, she would not look anyone in the eye lest the viewer should be killed or be turned into a green-eyed monster. This psychiatric case combines the Evil Eye concept with the projection theory of vision.

Compare this actual instance of psychopathology with an episode in the tales of the Brothers Grimm. In the tale "The Six Servants" a young prince has gone on a quest to win a princess, "the most beautiful maiden under the sun," by accomplishing a series of tasks set by her father. On his way he recruits six servants with

miraculous powers. The description of the fourth of these is as follows: "They traveled further and found a man sitting by the roadside who had his eyes blindfolded. The prince said to him, 'Have you weak eyes so that you can't see in the daylight?' 'No,' answered the man, 'I dare not take off the blindfold, for anything that I look on with my eyes shatters to bits; my glance is so powerful. If that can be of use to you I will serve you gladly.'

Later this servant rescues the princess by shattering the mountain within which she is imprisoned by her father and still later with a glance he destroys the armored knights sent to attack the prince's party.[14]

Folktale and mental illness tell the same story. They show how deeply embedded in the mind of man is the Evil Eye (even though it is working for the good guys in the folktale) and the projection theory of vision.

It stands to reason that if the Evil Eye is a universal concept, means to combat it must be similarly ubiquitous. This is true indeed. One could fill several volumes simply enumerating and illustrating the infinity of folk remedies, amulets, and talismans that have been employed through the millennia of human existence. For one interested in minutiae in this category there are three volumes published by Seligmann, while Hansmann and Kriss-Rettenbeck provide a beautiful pictorial exposition with many colored plates.[15]

The original reasoning behind some of the prophylactic measures is lost in the fogs of the past. However there are two major themes which are self-explanatory. One of these is the prophylactic eye amulet to ward off the Evil Eye. The eye amulet concept merges with that of the Apotropaic Eye and it will be reasonable to postpone discussion of eye amulets until chapters 3 and 4, where the two concepts are treated.

The other major identifiable notion behind Evil Eye amulets is that they must be offensive, obscene, or otherwise attention-getting. Thus in the numerous compounds of natural products urine, feces, and saliva play major roles, accompanied by herbs—especially repellent ones like garlic—and mud.

A very large number of amulets that operate via offensive repellency relate directly or metaphorically to the erect penis. In ancient Egypt the phallus amulet was a common one and most common of all was the *ankh*, the *crux ansata* (Fig. 3), whose origin in the phallus has been discussed in some detail by Elworthy.[16] In Roman times the universally used amulet hung around the neck of infants to protect them from the Evil Eye was the phallus combined with

Figure 3. Crux ansata in faience (Egypt)

Figure 5. Crude wooden *fascinum* (England). Fishbourne Roman Museum, Chichester, England. Photographed by author with permission.

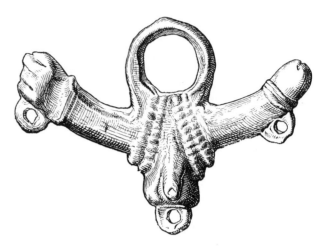

Figure 4. *Fascinum* or *turpicula res* (Rome). Otto Jahn, *Berichte über die Verhandlungen der Königlich sächsischen Gesellschaft der Wissenschaften zu Leipzig* 7 (1855):81.

a hand clenched with thumb protruding between the index and second fingers. This hand configuration is known in Italian as *mano fica* (Latin: *figere*; French: *ficher*) and was known in Latin as *manus obscena*. Its phallic significance is evident. The entire symbolism denotes potency and defiance simultaneously, and by folk logic it should be just the thing to avert the Evil Eye.

The combination of phallus and *mano fica* was labeled *turpicula res* (little shameful thing) by Varro, a man of letters of the first century B.C. (Fig. 4). It also was known as *fascinum* because of its amuletic powers against "fascination," that is, the Evil Eye. Although it existed in very large numbers throughout the Roman Empire in antiquity—one can see a crude example in wood from the first century A.D. in the Fishbourne Roman Museum outside Chichester in England (Fig. 5)—it all but disappeared thereafter. However, the *mano fica*, a symbol one step removed, has survived to the present and may still be bought in shops in southern Europe and in South America as protection against the Evil Eye. An assortment of examples may be seen in Figure 6.

A second step removed from the phallus, but still with unmistakably phallic intent, is the horn used as an amulet against the Evil Eye. In terms of numbers and distribution this is undoubtedly the most popular and most widely disseminated amulet today. Indeed, a common generic term in Italy for an amulet whether or not it represents a horn is *corno*. Materials vary from gold and silver through coral and abalone shell to red

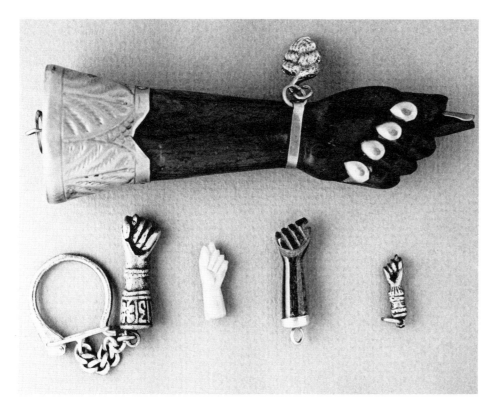

Figure 6. *Mano fica.* Large hand, above, in wood and brass (Brazil). Below, left to right, hands in silver (Brazil), coral (Naples), obsidian (Mexico), and silver (Rome).

Figure 7 (below). Horns as amulets. Top, amulets in dik dik horn (Rome), gold (Rome), silver (Atlantic City, N.J.), obsidian (Mexico), black plastic (Brazil), abalone shell (Mexico), silver (Naples). Below, amulet in silver and horn of uncertain species (North Africa). Bottom, amulet in red plastic with gilded crown (Palermo).

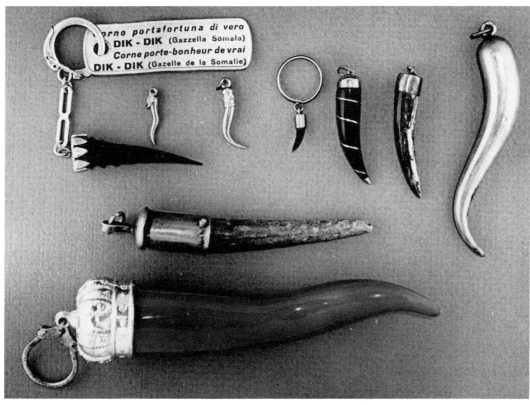

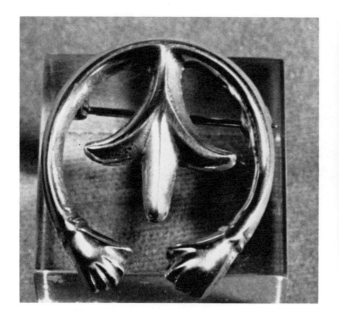

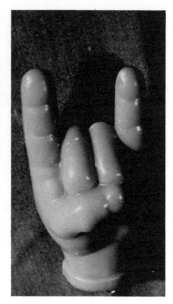

Figure 8. Navajo sand-cast silver naja, terminating in hands

Figure 9. *Mano cornuta* in plastic

plastic. Occasionally real horn is used. I once bought an amulet in the Rome airport that was labeled as authentic dik-dik horn (the dik-dik is a Somali gazelle). Sizes vary from the tiny sliver of gold for an infant's charm bracelet to ten-inch monsters that are particularly popular in shops and taxis. A series of horn amulets is shown in Figure 7.

By logical extension from the single horn, bicornuate amulets arise. By this route we move from bulls' horns over doorways, to horseshoes, to the crescent moon. A special case in this category is the *naja* of the Navajo silversmiths (Fig. 8). *Naja* is a Navajo word; but the thing it denotes, the pendant on the "squash blossom" necklace, is copied from the bicornuate amulet that appeared on the horse trappings of the Spanish conquistadores. Worn on the horse's forehead or sternum it protected horse and rider against the Evil Eye. However, one step farther into the past the Spanish borrowed this crescent amulet, usually terminated by a pair of hands as in our picture, from the Moors during the Arab domination of the Spanish peninsula. One additional step back, such an amulet is depicted on a Roman general's horse on Trajan's column.[17]

The bicornuate amulet may also be created by a hand sign, the *mano cornuta*. One extends the index and little finger holding the two middle fingers with the thumb. It is said that as a general precaution the citizen of a Mediterranean country who fears the Evil

Eye keeps a hand in his coat pocket forming the *mano cornuta*, but *in extremis* when faced with a known fascinator he may protect himself by pointing the "horns" directly at the eyes of the offender. The *mano cornuta* may also be purchased, usually in plastic, as an amulet (Fig. 9).

Before going farther into less obvious amuletic symbols it is time to call upon an authoritative witness from one of the allied fields we mentioned earlier. The field is psychiatry and the witness is none other than Sigmund Freud. Some of the most important scientific contributions of Freud are in his work on dreams. In this work much of his innovation lies in reading the symbolism used by the unconscious mind of the patient to create dream material. Freud was most explicit on the subject in his 1915–1916 lecture series given at the University of Vienna. His tenth lecture, "Symbolism in Dreams," contains the self-directed question, "We may enquire how we in fact come to know the meaning of these dream-symbols, upon which the dreamer himself gives us insufficient information or none at all." The answer follows: "My reply is that we learn it from very different sources—from fairy tales and myths, from buffoonery and jokes, from folklore (that is, from knowledge about popular manners and customs, sayings and songs) and from poetic and colloquial linguistic usage. In all these directions we come upon the same symbolism, and in some of them we can

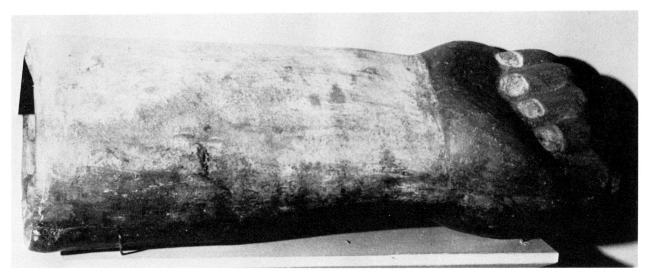

Figure 10. Hand (amulet?) from prehistoric site in Peru. Reproduced from author's photograph by permission, Field Museum of Natural History, Chicago.

understand it without further instruction. If we go into these sources in detail, we shall find so many parallels to dream-symbolism that we cannot fail to be con vinced of our interpretations."[18]

Farther along in the same lecture we find: "Likenesses of the male organ were regarded in antiquity as the most powerful *apotropaic* (means of defence) against evil influences, and, in conformity with this, the lucky charms of our own day can all be easily recognized as genital or sexual symbols. Let us consider a collection of such things—as they are worn, for instance, in the form of small silver hanging trinkets: a four-leaved clover, a pig, a mushroom, a horseshoe, a ladder, a chimney-sweep."[19]

Freud deals with each charm in the sequence and suggests its significance as a sexual symbol. It is interesting that the supportive evidence he adduces, most of it linguistic, identifies each charm as male or symbolizing nonspecific fruitfulness (the pig), except for the horseshoe, which in a lapse he calls female. The analysis above in which the horseshoe is identified as a bicornuate male horn is not only more credible to me but restores uniformity to the series.

Elsewhere in the same lecture we read: "Among the less easily understandable male sexual symbols are certain *reptiles* and *fishes,* and above all the famous symbol of the snake. . . . Finally we can ask ourselves whether the replacement of the male limb by another limb, the foot or the hand, should be described as sym-

bolic. We are, I think, compelled to do so by the context and by counterparts in the case of women."[20]

And finally this fragment: "and the *key* that opens it [door] is a decidedly male symbol."[21]

Thus in addition to our self-evident horns, Freud, on the basis of patient feedback, as well as on the basis of the folklore, jokes, and so on mentioned by him above, introduces a whole series of more remote male symbols. All of these have been used as amulets at some time.

Of particular interest is the hand. We have already seen how two hand configurations, the *mano fica* and the *mano cornuta*, enjoyed (and still enjoy) widespread use as prophylactics against the Evil Eye. Their significance as phallic symbols is immediately apparent and highly believable. There are numbers of other hand amulets, however, whose significance is less apparent without Freud's annotation. There are numbers of Egyptian hand amulets which consist either of hand with palm open and fingers extended but touching, or with fingers folded on the palm. This latter configuration is also seen on a pottery vessel from Peru now in the Field Museum (Fig. 10). Elworthy sketched numerous Etruscan amulets cut from sheet bronze, depicting the open hand with extended and separated fingers. He drew these from specimens in the Collegio Romano collection and in the museums of Cortona and of Bologna.[22]

Possibly a direct descendant of the Egyptian hand

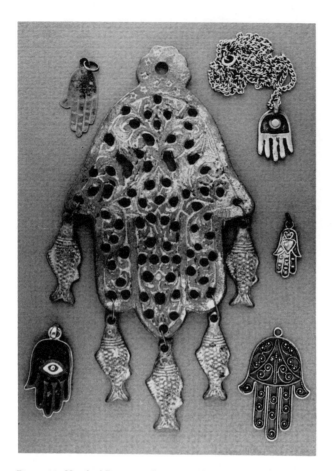

Figure 11. Hand of Fatima and variants. Large central hand with attached fish, in brass (Old City, Jerusalem). Upper left, silver hand (North Africa). Lower left, hand with eye in palm (Niello, Israel). Right edge, silver hands (all from North Africa although lower right was bought in Paris).

Figure 12. Hand with key and hand with snake (São Paulo, Brazil)

amulet is an item found in all Arab countries of the Middle East and particularly in North Africa. This is known as the hand of Fatima. Fatima was a daughter of Muhammad and was considered by him to be one of the "four perfect women." Her right hand is reproduced in silver in many forms. It is said to symbolize the whole of the Muslim religion and to be highly potent against the Evil Eye (Fig. 11).

Further strengthening of Freud's idea that snake and key are phallic symbols are two amulets I bought in São Paulo in 1966. One of these is a hand grasping a key, the second is a hand grasping a snake (Fig. 12). Keys alone and snakes alone are presented by Elworthy as amulets that he collected.[23]

The final piece of evidence to convince me that the hand is an intuitively recognized potent amulet (possi-

bly for Freud's reasons) rests in the existence of numerous and widely separated (in space and time) representations of the extended hand with eye in the palm—the hand-eye motif. One concentrated set of sites where this motif occurs is in the prehistoric remains of the Indians of the southeastern United States. A compendium of these occurs in Sun Circles and Human Hands by Fundaburk and Foreman. Moore and, more recently, Rands, have reported on the hand motifs of the area.[24] Two typical artifacts of the region are shown in Figures 13 and 14.

Add to this the demonstration by Schuster and Covarrubias that the same motif can be found in Peru, in Mexico, and among the Northwest Coast Indians (also see chapter 6) (Figs. 15–19). Finally, taking a large leap in space, there is in Thailand at least one instance of a hand of Buddha with a mandala inscribed in the eye position of the palm (Fig. 20). Jung equated the mandala with the eye on the basis of patients' drawings. This relationship is confirmed by the existence in a Tibetan lamasery near Lhasa of a sculptured image of "The White Tara"—a Buddha-like female deity of Lamaism. In the palm of each hand of this figure there is an actual eye. The potency and the connection of this combination must be basic and very intuitive.

There are several compound amulets which by the multiplicity of charms consolidated into one object must be considered to have special efficacy against the Evil Eye. In one of these the hand plays a central role again. This time the configuration is that of the *mano pantea*: thumb and first two fingers extended. Such an (unadorned) amulet was found in Pompeii and is now in the Naples museum, and the gesture was later associated with the priestly blessing or divine blessing in

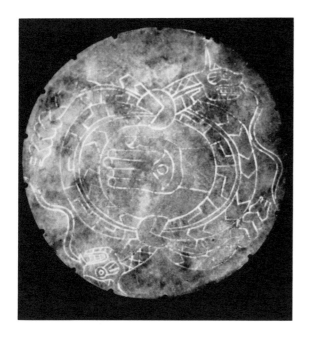

Figure 13. Hand-eye motif, here surrounded by snake. Pre-Columbian Indian stone plaque (southeastern U.S.). By permission of University of Alabama Museums, Moundville.

Figure 14. Hand-eye motif on pre-Columbian Indian incised pottery jar (southeastern U.S.). By permission of University of Alabama Museums, Moundville.

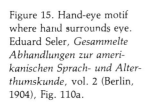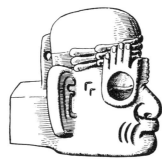

Figure 15. Hand-eye motif where hand surrounds eye. Eduard Seler, *Gesammelte Abhandlungen zur amerikanischen Sprach- und Alterthumskunde*, vol. 2 (Berlin, 1904), Fig. 110a.

Figure 16. Hand-eye motif. Aztec earth-god carved on stone box (Mexico). After Covarrubias, *The Eagle, the Jaguar, and the Serpent*. Original in Museum für Völkerkunde und Vorgeschichte, Hamburg.

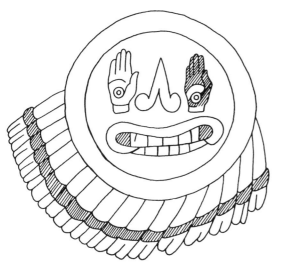

Figure 17. Hand-eye motif from "Lienzo de Tlaxcala" (Aztec-Spanish manuscript). Line drawing after Seler, *Gesammelte Abhandlungen zur amerikanischen Sprach- und Alterthumskunde*, Fig. 99.

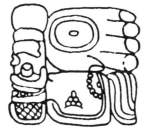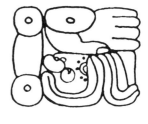

Figure 18. Hand-eye motif in "Maya Death Eyes." After J. E. S. Thompson, *Maya Hieroglyphic Writing: Introduction*, Pub. 589 of Carnegie Institution of Washington (Washington, D.C., 1950), Fig. 5. By permission of Carnegie Institution of Washington.

Figure 19. Hand-eye motif on Haida (Northwest Coast Indian) box. By permission of Field Museum of Natural History, Chicago.

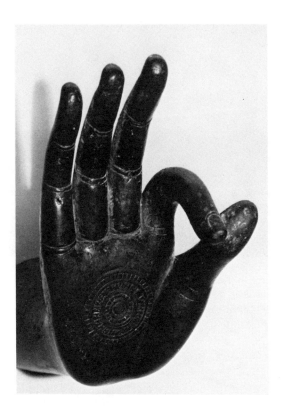

Figure 20. Hand of Buddha with mandala. By permission of Fine Arts Department, Bangkok, Thailand.

early Christian iconography. But the compound amulet of which we speak is a *mano pantea*, usually six to eight inches high, encrusted with numerous small amuletic figures. These figures usually include a knife, a serpent, a pinecone, a vase, a balance, a tortoise, a lizard, a frog, a scarab, a bust of Serapis, and a woman nursing a child; the representation of the various objects is fairly uniform in different amulets (Fig. 21). For a detailed discussion of the significance of each of these one should see the chapter on *mano pantea* in Elworthy. These hands apparently originate in the Roman Empire but Elworthy makes a strong case for most of the components being Egyptian. There is an attempt in the recent German literature to connect the hands with the cult of Sabazios (a surname of Bacchus, presumably of Thracian-Phrygian origin) and *Sabazios hand* is the designation used for the amulet by Hansmann and Kriss-Rettenbeck.[26] However this may be, the idea of multiple potency in a compound amulet comes through clearly.

A second compound amulet of more modern times is the *cima di ruta* or sprig of rue. This is a cast-silver pendant with a multibranching sprig. At the tip of each sprig is a shape of amuletic significance. These often include key, snake, crescent moon, hand, heart, cock, eagle, sword or dart, fish, and lotus. This amulet has no ancient counterpart. It reached its peak of production in Naples late in the nineteenth century and since has disappeared. A drawing of Elworthy depicts a typical *cima di ruta* (*cimaruta* in Naples) (Fig. 22).

Present-day short-cutting is apparent in the abbreviated combination amulets of hunchback and horns. The hunchback—Gobbo—is a common amulet dating from ancient times (see Elworthy).[27] Rubbing the hump of the hunchback has been thought by modern gamblers to bring them luck. More remotely one may ask as did Elworthy whether the predecessor of the hunchback is the Egyptian god Bes. One may also ask whether the Gobbo is related to Freud's chimney sweep. One form of the amulet has a white plastic hunchback suspended inside the red plastic horn. A second version has the white plastic hunchback holding a large red horn just before him. The reference to Priapus is obvious (Figs. 23, 24).

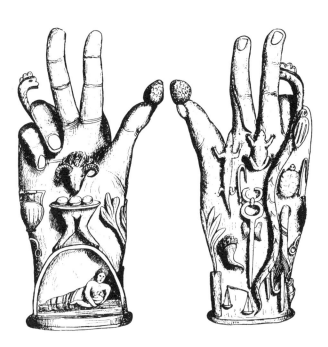

Figure 21. *Mano pantea* as compound amulet.
Elworthy, *The Evil Eye*.

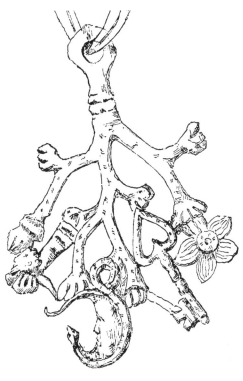

Figure 22. *Cima di ruta* or sprig of rue as
compound amulet. Elworthy, *The Evil Eye*.

Figure 23. Hunchback and horn

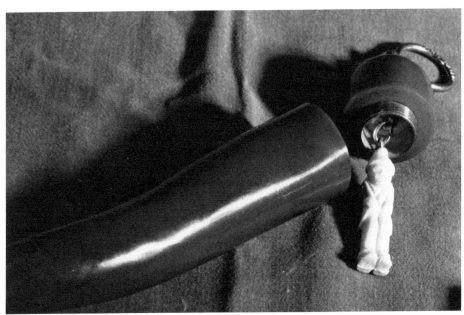

Figure 24. Hunchback and horn
in red and white plastic (Italy)

Figure 25. Jewish amulet. Seligmann, *Die Zauberkraft des Auges und das Berufen*.

Perhaps less interesting than the antic assortment of amulets above are two other types of prophylactic against the Evil Eye—the muttered formula and the written document. Under the gaze of a fascinator one has no time to think up snappy comebacks, so most muttered formulas are short prosaic affairs. In classic times *"Praefiscini"* was efficacious to ward off evil consequences; in Arab countries it was *"Mashalla."* In Jewish communities of central Europe *"Ken anhora"* (no Evil Eye) was the standard, as was *"Unberufen"* or *"Unbeschreien"* among German peasants.

Much more complex are the written charms used to avert the Evil Eye. These are particularly prevalent in the Middle East. Texts from the Koran in Arabic are often used, and here calligraphy sometimes plays a role in addition to content.[28] In Ethiopia written charms in the old Ethiopic language contained the mystical names of God, the names of the archangels, the names of fiends and devils, and so forth. Longer Ethiopic amulets contained miniature paintings of archangels and texts of magical tales.[29] Written amulets in Hebrew have had the widest subject range for they carry biblical passages, magic squares, and magic triangles. Many bear quotations from the *Book of Raziel*, a medieval book of magic. Perhaps the most widely disseminated of all of the written amulets come from the Cabala, a late medieval system of mysticism. An amulet with mostly cabalistic text, once in the possession of Seligmann, is shown here (Fig. 25). In this same category are amulets which have entered Orthodox Jewish religious observance. The doorpost of an Orthodox Jewish home carries in a holder of varying elaborateness a tiny parchment scroll bearing in Hebrew the passages Deut. 6:4–9 and 11:13–21. This scroll is called a mezuzah. The observant Orthodox Jew at his morning prayers wears a pair of phylacteries, one on the head and one on the left arm. These are small leather boxes held in position by leather thongs. The boxes contain strips of parchment with the two passages from Deuteronomy mentioned above along with Exod. 13:1–10 and 11–16. The amuletic origin of these practices is evident and the mezuzah had documented amuletic significance in talmudic times.[30] It is interesting to note that this type of use has returned. There is a trend among young Jewish girls today to wear the mezuzah as a pendant, though without conscious knowledge of its past and without conscious employment as an amulet.

One could go on for many pages but the purpose of this chapter has been accomplished. The welter of seemingly unconnected objects has been sorted out into some semblance of rational order, albeit a mad one, with a central concept. This concept was not devised by me for the occasion but is attested to by long generations of amulet fabricators from prehistory through ancient Rome to modern Naples and Sicily.

3. The Eye of Horus and Other Amulets

In the face of the all-pervading Evil Eye, what is more logical than the existence of a Good Eye—a countervailing force? If one did not exist, it would have to be created. The earliest known of all such eye amulets is the Eye of Horus, created by the ancient Egyptians. Tomb findings from the Fourth Dynasty onward include Eye of Horus amulets buried with the dead.[1] Thus the set of concepts encompassed by an eye amulet had to have been established by 2600 B.C., some forty-five centuries ago. Reasons for the preeminence of this particular symbolic eye are to be found in the myth of Horus as told in the Book of the Dead and the Pyramid Texts.

The Book of the Dead, which exists in fairly final form in second-millenium Egyptian papyri, is said by Budge to have existed in predynastic times (i.e., before 3100 B.C.) and is certain to have existed in some form during the First Dynasty (3100–2390 B.C.).[2] The Pyramid Texts were engraved on the walls and corridors of the pyramids at Saggara, which belong to the Fourth and Fifth Dynasties (ca 2613–2345 B.C.). Thus the legend is at least as old as the artifact.

Because of the cross-identification of the deities in Egyptian mythology, the story lines are more blurred than those of the European myths with which we are most familiar. A reasonably rational account of the Horus legend is the following: The two brothers Osiris and Set married their two sisters Isis and Nephtys. The jealousy between the two brothers soon manifested itself and Set enticed Osiris into being shut into a chest which was immediately thrown into the Nile. On learning this, Isis searched for the chest, found it, and hid it in a papyrus swamp before going off to seek help. Set, however, came upon the chest first, opened it, and dismembered the body. The parts were thrown to the four winds to prevent Isis from reassembling them and restoring her husband to life with her magic ring. The ibis-headed god Thoth came to the aid of Isis and the body was reassembled and vivified. Then Horus, son of Osiris and Isis, declared a war of revenge on Set and conquered him, but lost an eye in the battle. The Eye of Horus was restored by Thoth and thus became the symbol of the "sound-eye," that is, the Good Eye. The hieroglyph for this is called *utchat*.[3]

The artifact as found in ancient Egypt is obviously not a human eye or a variation on it. Horus was depicted as a hawk-headed god (Fig. 26), and the Eye of Horus amulet is a stylized hawk eye with the feather pattern of the predator playing a prominent role in the presentation (Fig. 27). Similarly the hieroglyph for the Eye of Horus differs from the hieroglyph for eye.

(Eye: Eye of Horus: .)

The Horus Eye amulet was made in faience, in stone, in precious metals, in enamels, and as inlay. It occurred as a single eye, a double eye, and even a quadruple eye (Figs. 28, 29).

Since in the Horus legend the eye was lost in the effort to avenge the father Osiris, the lost eye was thought of as a sacrifice for a father. By further extension the Eye of Horus became the symbol of all sacrifices and thus became one of the holiest symbols of the ancient Egyptian religion. Throughout Egyptian literature the phrase, "I give to thee the Eye of Horus" indicates the presentation of a sacrifice.[4]

This gives a notion of the breadth and depth of significance of the symbol. Next to the scarab it was the commonest symbol in ancient Egypt. The representation had several known funerary uses. It was placed in the mouth of the deceased. It was also placed upon the metal plate covering the left abdominal incision of the mummy through which the viscera had been removed. On the person of Tutankhamen there were no less than fourteen pieces of jewelry containing the Eye of Horus. Of these the pectoral ornament was an extremely elaborate piece of gold inlaid with lapis lazuli and other precious stones.[5]

Two Eyes of Horus were painted on the left side of the mummy coffin, opposite the head. This was so the deceased would have the power of looking out. Since the deceased was identified with Horus, he was able to see by means of the eye of the god (Fig. 30).

The unspecified Eye of Horus in the Pyramid Texts is always the left eye; however, the "two eyes" are also mentioned. In later symbolism these are equated with the sun and the moon. A legend current in ancient

Figure 26. Horus as hawk-headed god. By permission of Oriental Institute, University of Chicago (photograph no. 59789).

Figure 27. Typical Eye of Horus amulet. Drawing from author's paper "The Mind's Eye," *Quarterly Journal of the Cleveland Medical Library Association* 7 (1960):1. Reproduced by permission.

Figure 28. Eye of Horus amulets, single, double, and quadruple

Figure 29. Eye of Horus amulets. A representative assortment of styles, materials, and techniques.

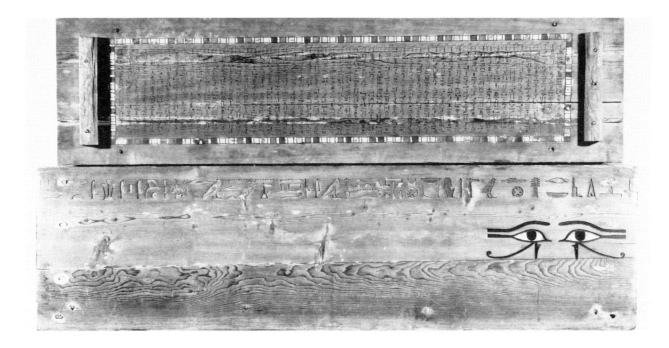

Figure 30. Egyptian wooden coffin of the Tenth Dynasty with the two Eyes of Horus. Oriental Institute, University of Chicago. Reproduced by permission (photograph no. 30144).

Egypt described the right eye as being swallowed by the goddess of heaven at nightfall, passing the night in her belly, and being born anew in the morning.

The eye painted on the ship's prow in Egypt was unmistakably the Eye of Horus, as tomb paintings, tomb sculptures, and papyri show (Fig. 31). The eye on the prow of a Sicilian fishing boat I saw drawn up on the coast at the site of the ancient Greek colony of Naxos might have been handed down from Egyptian to Greek to Sicilian in unbroken tradition. Only the distinctive features that identify the Eye of Horus had disappeared (Fig. 32). The eye on the prow of fishing boats persists in many Mediterranean countries. Here the significance lies somewhere between the eye amulet which we have described so far and the Apotropaic Eye described in the next chapter. As in many of the concepts with which we are dealing, multiple ideas are embodied in the same object. The weight of any given idea may vary with time, place, and user, but that the origin of this set of concepts is deep in antiquity is beyond debate.

A curious late derivative significance is attributed to the Eye of Horus. Apparently the symbol was fragmented as shown in Figure 33 by the pharmaceutical branch of the Egyptian priesthood. The pieces were used as mnemonics for a fractional series of measures of volume. When understood in this light the apparently mystical and unintelligible priestly "recitations" about the Eye of Horus make sense as a type of concealed formulary. The pieces of the ultimately stylized eye each represented a fraction with the numerator one.[6]

There is evidence that even in ancient times the Eye of Horus as amulet and as concept had become disseminated beyond the boundaries of Egypt. Several Horus Eyes were found by Petrie in a Philistine grave at Gezer. Others appear in Wooley's north Syrian cemetery of the Persian period and in the Phoenician graves explored by Johns at Atlit (ten miles south of present-day Haifa).[7] Interestingly, in each case stratified eye beads, which will be described below, were found too. Certainly other eyes of apparently amuletic significance have appeared in the Middle East. Cylinder seals bear identifiable eye symbols from the earliest times. Frankfort pictures several such seals from Syria as early as the Jemdat Nasr period (3100–2700 B.C.) or contemporary with the earliest Horus Eyes from Egypt.[8] Comparable but not so ancient eye symbols on a cylinder seal impression are shown in Figure 34.

Although the significance of eye beads (Fig. 35) as

Figure 31. Kephera in his boat (Egyptian papyrus). Note Eye of Horus on prow. Ernest A. T. Wallis Budge, *The Book of the Dead: The Papyrus of Ani*, vol. 1 (New York: G. P. Putnam's Sons, 1913), Pl. 10.

Figure 32. Sicilian fishing boat. Photograph made by the author near site of ancient Naxos.

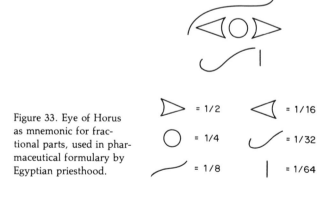

Figure 33. Eye of Horus as mnemonic for fractional parts, used in pharmaceutical formulary by Egyptian priesthood.

▷ = 1/2   ◁ = 1/16
○ = 1/4   ⌣ = 1/32
⌣ = 1/8 | = 1/64

eye amulets is not instantly convincing, the accumulated evidence leaves no alternative conclusion. Eisen in his definitive article tells how beads of this description were kept by the peasants of Brittany well into the twentieth century, how they had been preserved as heirlooms from remote centuries and were passed from hand to hand for the cure of various diseases. There has been no hesitation among modern archeologists who have dealt with the beads to identify them as eye beads.[9] The earliest datable eye beads belong to the Nineteenth Dynasty of Egypt (ca. thirteenth century B.C.), almost fifteen centuries after the first appearance of the Eye of Horus. They were made in Africa and Europe by four general techniques from that time through the Venetian Renaissance. Their constant association with the Eye of Horus, often on the same necklace, within Egypt and elsewhere in the Middle

Figure 34. Rhombic eye symbol on Mittanian cylinder seal from the middle of the second millenium B.C.

Figure 35 (below). Ancient eye beads used as amulets

East strongly suggests that they represent the ultimate in abbreviation combined with multiplexing (as described in chapter 6) and were intended to represent the Eye of Horus. The tendency to multiplication is already manifest in the quadruple eye of Figure 29 and a twenty-eyed piece of Petrie's.[10]

The four types of manufacturing technique are:

1. Simple eye spots, made by applying a small mass of a contrasting color of glass to the basic bead. These were the simplest and earliest.
2. Painted eye rings, in which rings were pressed into clay beads before firing, and the impressions were filled with pigment to give the appropriate effect of sclera, iris, and pupil; on occasion two rings represented sclera and an iris-pupil combination. All the beads with painted eye rings were quite early. Some exemplars are seen in Figure 35.
3. Stratified rings, manufactured by superimposing small circular layers of colored glass on the basic glass bead to represent sclera, iris, and pupil in that order. Some of the eye beads of the Nineteenth Dynasty tombs are of this type. Figure 35 includes some examples.
4. Inlaid coils, the most sophisticated technique, in which glass canes made up of concentric or spiral layers of glass are cut in cross section. When the rod is viewed end-on, an eye effect is perceived. Small pieces of these rods were fused into depressions in the main bead to make numerous eyes. This is the "millefiori" technique, used in Egypt from the time of the Ptolemies; most familiar in Venetian glass, it is still in use today. No ancient exemplars were

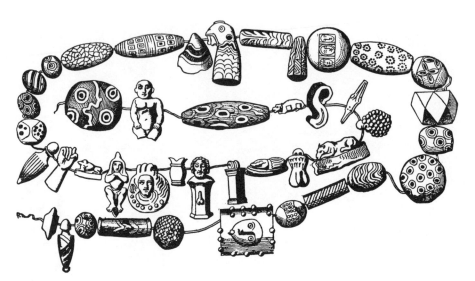

Figure 36. Eye beads strung with other ancient amulets against the Evil Eye. Achik, *Antiquités du Bosphore Cimmèrien.*

Figure 37 (below). Amuletic eye bead (modern Greece)

available but a modern illustration of this technique appears in Figure 37.

Still in the eye bead category there is the string of amulets first reported by Achik (Fig. 36) where eye beads are interspersed with the standard amulets of the Roman period such as phallus, Priapus, toad, and *mano fica*. The dating of this type of find is most difficult since it is improbable that any of the beads were made at the site of the find. The component beads could all be of late Egyptian or middle Roman manufacture, or some could be intrusions preserved from a much earlier period.[11]

In modern times the most widespread eye amulets are the glass eyes that are everywhere in the eastern Mediterranean and Asia Minor. Judging by the distribution in all of the countries once under Ottoman dominion it appears that the Turkish influence is central, but this is a surmise on my part rather than a studied conclusion. Certainly the central bazaar in Istanbul appears to be the world center for these items, although they are common also in Greece and among Israeli Arabs. The glass eyes vary in execution from a simple white circle surrounded by a yellow circle on a flat blue bead (Fig. 37) (this one is hung around the necks of infants in the Athens region), to carefully painted, gold- or silver-mounted objects, with white scleras, blue irises, and black pupils (Fig. 38). They vary in size from minuscule to enormous and in number from one to ten or more in the same mount (Fig. 39).

The prominent Turkish ophthalmologist Dimir Basar told me that in his country a particularly effica-

cious combination against harm was thought to be an eye amulet and a gold coin. Many a boy was sent off to school with this necessary equipment. Recognition of the value of this combination is seen in Figure 40 even though in my piece from the Istanbul bazaar the coin is very thin base metal with surface gilding.

All these eye amulets have blue irises. There are two reasons for this. First, a blue iris is never seen in the dark-skinned populations of the Mediterranean. It would thus be rare, exotic, and foreign. Secondly, the color blue has an amuletic potency of its own in these regions. The most direct illustration of this is the prevalence of strings of bright blue beads of crude pottery hung around the necks of large domestic animals as amulets. Known in the United States under the

Figure 38. Assorted eye amulets, each with blue iris (Turkey)

Figure 39 (below). Eye amulets characterized by multiple eyes and variable size (Turkey)

Figure 40 (left). Eye amulet and gold coin, a Turkish tradition

Figure 41 (right). "Donkey beads," originally used to protect domestic animals from Evil Eye

Figure 42. Eye amulet from Armenian pottery in Jerusalem

Figure 43. Eye agates or Aleppo stones

Figure 44. *Ojo de venado* or
deer's eye amulet (Mexico)

generic term of "donkey beads," they have been adopted to some extent by the current counterculture (Fig. 41).

It is not difficult to suppose that all of the eye beads
and eye amulets, including the modern ones, derive
from the Eye of Horus and that they entered Muslim
life from the fragments of Roman and Egyptian culture
assimilated by the Arab conquests.

In addition to all of the amulets already mentioned
there are a few which because of material or design are
of particular note. One of these I first saw above the
door of a shop in the Old City of Jerusalem. On inquir-
ing foolishly whether it was for sale, I was told with an
indulgent smile that it was not; it belonged to the shop.
Its counterpart (Fig. 42) comes from the Armenian pottery by the Damascus Gate. In addition to the blue iris
it has a curious break in the roundness of the pupil
known to ophthalmologists as a pupillary coloboma.
Rarely such a coloboma occurs as a congenital defect,
but when it does it is always found directly below, in
the six o'clock position. The coloboma in this protec-
tive eye is at one o'clock and can only be the result of
surgery or accidental trauma. Nevertheless, it serves
along with the blue iris to make this an eye amulet of
special potency to ward off misfortune from the shop
in the Old City.

An eye amulet in the same spirit as the eye beads
but distinguished by its unusual material is known as

the eye agate or *Aleppo stone* (Fig. 43). If a piece of
agate whose layers happen to fall with appropriate
spacing is cut as a circular cabochon (or round dome)
with the base parallel to the direction of the layers, one
can achieve an eyelike effect. When viewed from
above, the stone presents a dark outer ring surrounding white ring which in turn surrounds a dark center
circle. These convincingly eyelike stones are mounted
in numerous ways to form complete amulets.

Finally in the miscellaneous eye amulet category
comes the assortment of natural products that are eyelike and have been adapted as amulets. These are usually beans or other seeds. The example shown here
(Fig. 44) is a large brown seed with a dark germinal
stripe. It is native to Mexico and is known there as *ojo
de Venado* (deer's eye). In this instance it is strung with
wool tufts, pieces of wood of unidentified nature, am-
berlike yellow beads, and pink coral to form a potent
amulet against the Evil Eye.

The preceding material should be enough to convince even a skeptic that not only is the Evil Eye concept a fundamental human idea, basic to man's nature
since before recorded history, but that the eye amulet
is just as ancient, just as pervasive, just as persistent.
It, too, belongs somewhere at the bottom of the trunk
as one of the earliest and most basic pieces of human
emotional baggage.

4. The Eye of Medusa

The horrible Gorgon, Medusa, the very sight of whom turned every living thing to stone, is one of the well-established figures of Western mythology. As it happens, the Gorgon story and its representations in art are pivotal in explaining a world-pervading idea about the eye that has dwelt in man's mind since prehistoric times. As far back as we can get any glimmer of thought, this idea—the concept of the Apotropaic Eye—has existed. It is still very much alive in many parts of the world today, and the explanatory threads which lead back from antiquity to prehistory and forward to the present day radiate out from the Gorgon of classical Greece.

The word apotropaic is from the Greek *apo* (away from) and *trope* (turn). That which is apotropaic has the power of turning away evil; it is aversive. The object with this power is an *apotropaion*. An excellent perspective on this concept comes from Jane Harrison's remarkable book, *Prolegomena to the Study of Greek Religion*. As Harrison and fellow members of the "Cambridge School" have shown, there are clear indications in Greek literature and art of a primitive substratum to the worship of the well-known gods of Olympus—Zeus, Hera, Aphrodite, Hermes, and the rest. This primitive religion whose memory had been suppressed even as early as Homeric times was a set of gloomy exercises preserved in special seasonal holidays of classical times. The Lupercalia of Rome mentioned in Shakespeare's *Julius Caesear* was one of these. Another was the primitive worship of the "chthonic deities" later personified as Demeter and Dis. The one unifying feature of this primitive pre-Olympian religion was its apotropaic function—the turning away of evil spirits which might be ghosts of the dead or any of the myriad specific bogeys such as the Keres, Harpies, Fates, or Furies. This is in sharp contrast to the characteristics of the Olympian religious practices which involved cultivation (*therapeia*) of the gods.[1] The flourishing of apotropaic religious practices required apotropaic objects as amulets. An important *apotropaion* has always been the representation of a menacing face associated with so much horror that it drives evil away from its owner. The most expressive part of the face, the eye, also has apotropaic potency.

The apotropaic concept is one vital part of the three-part combination I have labeled the "Watchbird concept complex."[2] Here the watcher is so horrible in appearance that he turns away evil from the watched.

There is little need to reiterate the classical Gorgon myth, fixed in its final form long before the time that Ovid retold it in the first two decades B.C. The story of how the sleeping Medusa was beheaded by Perseus while watching her reflection in his polished shield; how the severed head retained its potency and turned the enemies of Perseus to stone when they gazed on its uncovered horror; how Perseus finally presented the head to Athene who placed it in the center of her shield (the aegis) is still known to every schoolchild.[3]

The prominent role that the Gorgon, and particularly the Gorgon head, played in Greek decorative art is less widely known, although it has been the subject for extensive scholarly study and numerous publications. Two reviews that sum up the thought of the last hundred years are those of Furtwängler and of Howe. Much has been made of how the Gorgon first appeared in Greek art in the eighth century, then became disseminated through the Greek world, and in the course of time underwent a change in nature.[4]

As an adequate measure of wideness of geographical distribution one can examine the occurrence of the Gorgon on ancient coins. This is particularly appropriate since one of its first representations in Greek art is thought to be on an eight-century electrum stater of Parium—a settlement on the south shore of the Propontis, about a hundred miles west of present-day Istanbul.[5] At least thirty-seven localities in the ancient world struck coins showing the head of Medusa. These stretched from Italy to the Black Sea (see Appendix A). A typical Gorgoneion coin is seen in Figure 45.

With only rare exceptions (Neapolis, Parium) the Gorgon could be considered the standard symbol for the locality as Athene and the owl were coin types for Athens. Nevertheless, the wide dissemination represents a popularity for Gorgon coins second only to those representing the major Olympian deities. It seems reasonable to attribute this to the apotropaic powers of the Gorgon. What could be better than to have a coin that was at the same time money and an

Figure 45. Gorgoneion of archaic style on coin of Neapolis, Macedon, fourth to fifth century B.C.

Figure 46. Typical archaic Gorgoneion. Antefix from Acropolis (Athens). Ross, *Archaeologische Aufsätze*, Pl. 8.

amulet? This is a logical explanation of the wideness of distribution and the popularity of the Gorgon coins.

It is also clear that the earliest representations emphasized the horrible aspects of the Gorgon. The exaggeratedly round face, the staring eyes, the menacing teeth, were all constant features. The snakes at waist, neck, or hair and the protruding tongue were nearly constant features. An exemplar of this early type of representation is shown in Figure 46.

Toward the middle of the fifth century the type began to be modified. The features became less menacing, the snakes grew more stylized, and the boar tusks disappeared. Many exemplars of this modified Gorgon appear on coins and on the shields of warriors depicted in vase paintings. Figure 47 shows such a middle-period representation. Finally, after another century, the humanizing and beautifying effects of Greek art worked their total change and Medusa was transformed into a beautiful woman. The example given by all writers on the subject—and it is easy to understand why—is the Medusa Rondanini (Fig. 48). This beautiful and classic marble, probably a copy of an earlier bronze original, was discovered by Goethe in the Palazzo Rondanini in Rome. For a complete exposition of the evolution of the Medusa concept in art, see the article by Wilson. Buschor has excellent pictures and emphasis on the last phase.[6]

Figure 47. Gorgoneion of intermediate type on hemidrachm of Parium, fourth century B.C.

Figure 48. Gorgon head of classical beauty, "Medusa Rondanini." Photograph by Theodor Heller. Glyptothek, Munich. Reproduced by permission.

Figure 50. Plate showing Medusa with body of Artemis as Mistress of Wild Things (Camiros, Rhodes). Six, "Some Archaic Gorgons in the British Museum," Pl. 59.

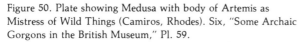

Figure 49. Archaic Medusa with female body. Metope from Temple C, Selinunte. Photograph by the author.

Figure 51. Gorgon with Harpy body. Archaic vase in Berlin Museum. Engelmann, "Harpyie," p. 211.

Figure 52. Gorgon with body of centaur, beheaded by Perseus. Neck of pithos (vase).
De Ridder, "Amphores beoticnnes à reliefs," Pl. 4.

There is a very specific purpose in giving this degree of detail on the evolution of the Medusa concept. It is to emphasize that the early and basic concept was the horror-creating apotropaic figure. The later versions which were domesticated by the Greek artistic genius and which deviated from the original intention are measures of the civilized nature of later Greek culture but lose the original apotropaic force of the Gorgon.

It is worth noting, too, that in archaic Greek art and in the earlist literature the representation was invariably the Gorgoneion—the Gorgon head. It is a striking phenomenon that each of the allusions to the Gorgon in Homer (only four in all) refers to the Gorgon head alone, the Gorgoneion without a specified body.[7]

It was too much to ask of the Greeks that they should not later supply a body to Medusa, but they were neither comfortable nor consistent about the body they did supply. Some of the late archaic representations were of a standard female body as in the metope from Temple C at Selinunte (Fig. 49) or the relief from the sixth-century temple at Corfu. However,

on a plate from Camiros in Rhodes (Fig. 50), the unmistakable Gorgon head is attached to a body whose hands hold two swans. This is an early Artemis in her role as Mistress of Wild Things (potnia theron). On the vase in the Berlin Museum there is a Gorgon with a Harpy body in the act of snatching two children (Fig. 51). On the neck of another archaic vase from Boeotia is a beheading-of-the-Gorgon scene complete with Perseus averting his gaze. Here, however, the Gorgon has the body of a centaur (Fig. 52).[8] The explanation given by several scholars is a satisfying one: that in the area where this vase was manufactured there was a cult of Poseidon as god of horses rather than exclusively god of the sea. He was called Poseidon Hippios by Aeschylus (Seven against Thebes, line 130). It is appropriate then that the one of his consorts from whose blood the winged horse Pegasus sprung should have equine characteristics.

The point of all this is to emphasize that the functional original Gorgon was the gruesome apotropaic mask with no body at all. The very earliest examples,

Figure 53. Clay head of animallike Gorgon found at Tiryns. After Hampe, *Frühe Griechische Sagenbilder in Böotien.*

Figure 54. Clay mask (Nippur). Oriental Institute, University of Chicago. Reproduced by permission (photograph no. 2N-513).

the coin of Parium and the clay head found at Tiryns (Fig. 53), fulfill these criteria. For other instances, see Payne's *Necrocorinthia.*[9] In literature during the fifty to seventy-five years between Homer and Hesiod and in art between the proto-Corinthian and Corinthian periods (late eighth to early seventh century) the Greek Gorgon acquired a female body of some sort, and the Perseus legend was generated. Note particularly that whatever the details of the legend, the inevitable denouement—decapitation—served to sever the Gorgon head from its poorly fitting body and to regenerate the Gorgoneion mask which retained its apotropaic powers.

The Gorgoneion was unknown in Mycenaean art and during the Geometric period. It appeared in Greece relatively suddenly and relatively well characterized at the end of the eighth century. Where did it originate?

Many indications point to Babylonia and Assyria. One such indication lies in the pattern of coin distribution. Not only does the oldest coin (Parium) come from Asia Minor but the highest concentration of Gorgoneion coins is in the Greek colonies that lie on the shores of the Anatolian peninsula.

Another powerful indicator is the series of clay

Figure 55. Sketch of impression from Babylonian cylinder seal, perhaps of Ionian origin. Ward, *The Seal Cylinders of Western Asia*, no. 643.

Figure 56 (below). Gorgon figure in "knielaufen" position. A. Furtwängler and K. Reichhold, *Griechische Vasenmalerei* (Munich: F. Bruckmann, 1900), Pl. 1.

head masks found in Babylonian and Assyrian sites. They all have exaggeratedly round faces, grinning sinister smiles, and menacing teeth. Many were found hanging on the walls of tombs, with an obviously apotropaic intent. Van Buren in her catalog lists twenty-seven and Thureau-Dangin speaks of seeing others in the hands of dealers. Thus this apotropaic demon mask must have been commonplace in Babylonia and Assyria. They continue to be found. A fairly recently excavated member of this series is shown in Figure 54. Reported by the University of Chicago Nippur expedition in 1967, it comes from the Third Dynasty of Ur period—about 2000 B.C.[10] Many would like to see these clay masks as the head of Humbaba, the demon who was conquered by the hero Gilgamesh in the famous Babylonian epic. It is not very important for our purposes whether this is true or not and indeed there is no documentary evidence to connect Babylonian iconography with the scanty written material. However, the argument offered by Sidney Smith on the basis of an inscribed divination plaque that no Humbaba is authentic without an entrail face is certainly fallacious. What we do have in the clay plaques is an early Mesopotamian equivalent of the Gorgoneion which could well be its precursor.[11]

To extend the parallelism, several cylinder seals exhibit decapitation scenes strongly reminiscent of Perseus and the Gorgon. On these seals the monster is male as are the "Humbaba" heads above. On one cylinder in particular (Ward, no. 643) the parallelisms are striking. The monster-victim (Humbaba?) has a large bristly head shown full-face and is in a characteristic position with one knee and the foot of the other leg on the ground (Fig. 55). This "knielaufen position" is not only common on the pertinent oriental cylinder seals (Ward, nos. 642, 643, 644, 646) but is also common in archaic Greek representations of the Gorgon. Figure 56 shows such a Greek Gorgon. The case for the origins of the Gorgon in the Middle East and specifically in the Humbaba demon is put most effectively by Hopkins in a seventeen-page article with copious illustrations.

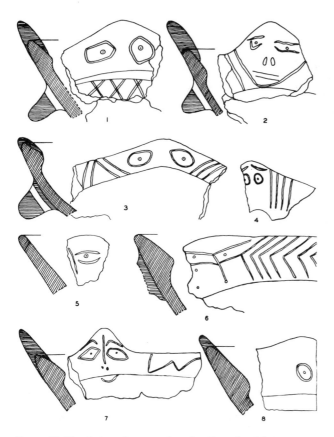

Figure 57. Shards from face-pots found at Troy (level I). Blegen et al., *Troy*. Reprinted by permission of Princeton University Press.

Figure 58. Shards from face-pots found at Stentinello, Sicily. Museo Archaeologico, Syracuse. Reproduced by permission.

Note, too, that in the Cypriot cylinder (Ward, no. 643) the head of the hero-executioner is averted and his weapon is the curved sickle-shaped *harpé* of the Middle East. Curiously, on an archaic Greek vase the Gorgon has the "knielaufen" position and the Perseus carries the alien *harpé*—a strong suggestion of oriental origin for the legend itself. All the above says that the ancients of the Near East were as uncomfortable with their synthesized demon as the Greeks were with theirs. In each case the decapitation regenerated an apotropaic mask—in Babylonia and Assyria, the "Humbaba" mask; in Greece, the Gorgoneion.[12]

There is good evidence that the apotropaic face extends far back into prehistory. Blegen's report on the University of Cincinnati excavations at Troy discloses that every level from the fifth back to the first contained pots with faces on sides, tops, or handles as their principal motif. At each level the execution was in the common technique of the period. Thus the earliest examples, those from Troy I, had crudely incised but completely recognizable faces (Fig. 57). Blegen's dates for this period are 3000–2500 B.C.—prehistoric indeed for anywhere on earth. Face-pots continued to appear at Troy until 1800 B.C.. That they had apotropaic significance must be inferred, but the inference is a strong one. There are prehistoric parallels elsewhere and there is the striking existence of the eye kylix to be dealt with below.[13]

A prehistoric parallel in the Mediterranean is found in the Stentinello pottery of Sicily. In the fourth millennium, actually preceding Troy I, pots with crudely incised eyes, some with lashes, a few with noses, were made at this site near Syracuse. Some shards are depicted in Figure 58. There can be little reasonable doubt of the apotropaic function of these face-pots made more than 5,000 years ago.[14]

The merest fragment of a pot from Stone Age China has painted on it an eye with lashes, very much like the Stentinello eyes and equally emphatic in purpose.[15]

Still another example of prehistoric face-pots, later in time but truly prehistoric, are those of pre-Columbian Peru. While a number of Peruvian pieces are cinerary urns and represent effigies of real or imagined persons, this is not the series that concerns us. There are numerous Peruvian pottery cups, however, from both the north and south coast on which only heads are depicted. The heads range from completely animal, such as the feline head represented in Figure 59, to nearly human, such as that in Figure 60. Even in the latter example, bared teeth or feline fangs or lolling

Figure 59. Peruvian face-pot with feline characteristics, early Paracas period. By permission of Metropolitan Museum of Art, New York (gift of Nathan Cummings 62.266.72).

Figure 60 (below). Peruvian face-pot with nearly human characteristics, formative Paracas period. By permission of Metropolitan Museum of Art, New York (gift of Nathan Cummings 62.266.72).

Figure 61. Carved gourd from Huaca Prieta, Peru. Probably antecedent of the face-pots. After Junius B. Bird, "Excavations in Northern Chile," Anthropological Papers of the American Museum of Natural History, vol. 38, pt. 4 (1943).

Figure 62 (below). Face-pot from the Melanesians of the Sepik River. By permission of Field Museum of Natural History, Chicago.

tongue allow no mistake about the apotropaic purpose of the decoration. Indeed the very earliest Peruvian vessel, not a piece of pottery but a carved gourd (Fig. 61), carries such a face. It is dated at 2500–2000 B.C.[16]

In true proof of universality one can cite a contemporary primitive example of the face-pot. There is very little pottery in Melanesia, but in one area, along the Sepik River of northwest New Guinea, there has been a moderately sophisticated pottery industry which was found by the earliest Western explorers. Reche in his Hamburg Museum expedition of 1908–1910 photographed a number of face-pots, and the Basel Museum Expedition of 1956 found the tradition still going strong. Several Sepik River face-pots are in the Field Museum collection and are shown in Figures 62 and 63. These are much closer to Troy I and to Stentinello than they are to Greek black-figured vase painting, but the purpose is unmistakable. They are apotropaic in a strong tradition, for we can document their persistence for half a century in the face of the most severe intrusions of Western culture. Their thematic origin in antiquity, or in the recesses of the mind common to all mankind, can only be guessed at.[17]

One cannot treat the Gorgon without mentioning the stone relief found at Chavín de Huántar in the central Peruvian Andes by Ayres. No causative relationship is implied, but it can be seen from Figure 64 that

Figure 63. Sepik River face-pot. By permission of Field Museum of Natural History, Chicago.

all of the Gorgon attributes are present—the feline fangs, the snaky hair, and the human erect stance—a thoroughly apotropaic figure, half a world away and perhaps half a century before the Gorgon came to ancient Greece.[18]

It was said earlier that the Gorgon concept was the most highly developed embodiment from which the Apotropaic Eye could be thought to extend from prehistory to the present. If this is true, the very heart of that embodiment is the Gorgon kylix.

The kylix is a drinking cup with a low bowl and a supporting foot and was a standard shape for Greek potters. Every moderately well-to-do household must have owned a number of them. Kylices were not the first pottery shapes to bear paintings of the Gorgoneion—other vase shapes of proto-Corinthian pottery were so painted as early as the late eighth century. Neither were the early kylices decorated with Gorgoneia. However, during the last half of the sixth century the Gorgon kylix appeared in Athens and rocketed to popularity (Fig. 65). The most popular arrangement and the one that concerns us had a Gorgoneion painted on the inside of the bowl. On the outside

Figure 64. The Gorgon of Chavín. Gorgon-like figure from Peru, antedating the Greek Gorgon. After Ayres, "Rubbings from Chavín de Huántar, Peru."

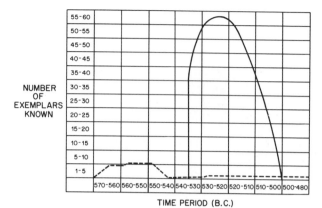

Figure 65. Introduction of the Gorgon motif into Greek vase painting. After Muick, "Gorgoneia in Attic Painting." By permission of Mr. Muick.

Figure 66 (above). Interior surface of typical Gorgon kylix. By permission of Metropolitan Museum of Art, New York.

Figure 67 (left). Outer rim of Gorgon kylix shown in Fig. 66. Note typical Apotropaic Eyes. By permission of Metropolitan Museum of Art, New York.

of the bowl were one or two pairs of enormous eyes. Two typical examples are in the Metropolitan Museum Collection of the University of Chicago (Figs. 66–69). In a 1955 thesis, Muick cataloged the published Gorgon kylices. He listed 134 kylices which have both the Gorgon within and the eyes outside. This should give some notion of the profusion of such cups which must have existed in antiquity.[19]

The message that these cups carry is easily read. The apotropaic force of the head of Medusa inside the cup can be abstracted and placed on the outside using the eyes—the most essential feature—alone. Thus the eyes alone, particularly when enlarged, carry the full apotropaic force. The virtue of an apotropaion on a drinking cup to ward off evil from the drinker need not

be belabored. Finally, on an even greater number of kylices and to a lesser extent on cups of other shapes (the kyathos for example) the Gorgon no longer appears and only the Apotropaic Eyes remain. These eye kylices were sufficiently abundant that they are still purchasable from the better private dealers. They must have been made in truly enormous qualities.[20]

If the eye kylix represents the Eye of Medusa in its most direct and concretized apotropaic potency, the Apotropaic Eye itself is by no means so restricted in time and place. Once more we are dealing with a basic human concept found in all parts of the globe and in all times from prehistory to the present. The foregoing is but a part of the story. Wider dissemination of the Apotropaic Eye is described in the following chapters.

Figure 68. Interior of kylix showing smaller Gorgon head. By permission of Metropolitan Museum of Art, New York.

Figure 69. Exterior rim of Gorgon kylix of Fig. 68. Very large Apotropaic Eyes persist here. By permission of Metropolitan Museum of Art, New York.

5. Behind the Mask

If the Gorgoneion is the prime exemplar of the Apotropaic Eye, what about masks, particularly primitive masks? Aren't they apotropaic too? My answer is an emphatic albeit qualified yes.

The first thing to realize is that masks like most primitive cultural creations are not the result of a logical hypothesis brought to a logical conclusion. They are the result of half-thoughts and inner feelings of extreme complexity, brought to embodiment from the deepest recesses of the soul. Their origins are multiple and complex. Their meanings are many, multivariant, and frequently overlapping. Only a very naïve reductionist will say that primitive masks represent any single thing or concept.

An excellent view of the mask problem is given by C. A. Valentine in his *Masks and Men in a Melanesian Society*.[1]

Except for the plains of North America, the islands of Polynesia, and the continent of Australia, there is hardly a major world area in which masks are absent or unimportant.

Prehistoric evidence suggestive of masking goes back to the paintings of the Paleolithic, and a long train of later archeological and historical forms leads up to the latest models available from costume suppliers and novelty shops.

Not only is the mask continuous from prehistory but it can represent animals, birds, monsters, inanimate objects, human features, or true abstractions.

Valentine goes on to emphasize the transcending quality of masks when seen as objects and particularly when worn for their intended purpose.

The feeling arises that a masked performer has somehow undergone a metamorphosis and assumed in living form the qualities of his disguise. The watching audience knowing that what it sees is a person wearing something which he can again take off, nevertheless is captured by the illusion that the mask somehow belongs to the figure and expresses its nature. Wearers of masks, on the other hand, often report that they feel more or less transformed by the image they are wearing, so that they are moved to act according to the characteristics which are associated with it.

The author suggests that this force comes partly from the fact that a person is recognized by his face, and that a false face with or without body costume transforms the individual to a new and strange character.

These fundamental illusions are usually heightened still further by various ways in which the tradition of mystification surrounding maskery and mummery is perpetuated. The circus audience is not ordinarily allowed to see the clown take off his false face, nor do modern masked actors usually remove their disguises in public. In Africa or New Guinea the uninitiated are often told that the masked figures *are* the spirits which they impersonate, and those not admitted to the mysteries are never allowed to see the masks being taken off. So in one way or another the transformation from the masked figure to the ordinary man is hidden from the public gaze, and thus the mysterious distinction between the two is preserved. Also the construction of the mask itself and the way in which it is worn or fastened to the head are usually more or less private knowledge, restricted to those who wear and make the disguises. The importance of these props of mystery can also be seen in the fact that the revelation of their true nature to members of privileged groups usually involves some degree of crisis for the individuals involved and may be highly ritualized. Puberty rites among many peoples involve the acquisition of such knowledge. Revelations of this kind are appropriately described as "unmasking." Masks retain much of their effectiveness just because this is normally allowed to happen only in special circumstances such as growing out of childhood or becoming a member of an esoteric group.

Though one recognizes multiplicity of motive and of transformation by the mask, one is still entitled to try to examine as far as possible some of the individual threads that are twisted into this complex and knotted cord. Here as nowhere else the caveats mentioned in the introductory chapter obtain. Anthropologists did not ask many of the questions we want answered. When they did ask such questions, the almost universal connection of masks with primitive secret societies prevented them from getting truthful answers. Since motivations are multiple and partly unconscious, the maskers are frequently unable to give meaningful answers even if they wish to. By the time investigators make any real contact with a people, there has been subtle and unsubtle Western cultural contamination so that a sense of shame about the darker parts of the masks and accompanying ritual prevent honest communication. Finally there is the current tendency in anthropology, due to the influence of the more exact sciences, to avoid even stating hypotheses if they are not subject to rigorous proof. This is most commendable and precludes much nonsense and lunatic clutter in the literature. The net result, though, is that one is left with little more than the artifacts themselves.

Here then is one of those situations in which the reader is merely asked whether the hypotheses advanced seem credible. If the answer is yes, we have reached the limited objective of this essay. Our hypothesis in this case is that there is a large and significant apotropaic element among the diverse psychological dynamic elements that are responsible for the creation of masks.

On the basis of late-nineteenth-century anthropology, the psychologist Wilhelm Wundt had very definite ideas about the primitive mask. In his *Völkerpsychologie* he speaks of fantasy in primitive art and the fusion of animal and human features.[2]

This is exhibited particularly strikingly in the masks which occur in the most widely separated localities around the globe. Originally these were usually components of a religious cult. Then they were used everywhere to inspire terror. Since this was achieved by asserting that a demon was concealed behind the mask, the religious origin persisted. Finally when this change of significance completely disappeared, the mask simply served the purpose of playful masquerade. If one looks beyond the skull masks which frequently occur in the earlier stages and beyond the animal heads and their representations where the form is predetermined, the creation of masks is that branch of primitive art in which fantasy is exercised in the wildest combinations.

Wundt's figure 20 shows actual examples of transition from predominantly animal to predominantly human features in masks. However, animal characteristics survive in the widely opened mouth and the staring eyes. These characteristics appear in pictorial art and convey the terror generated by demons and avenging spirits. The greater the terror the more animallike are the features. Wundt goes on: "An eloquent example is the Gorgon type in its transformations undergone in the course of time. The oldest representations recall the horrible animal masks of the primitives. To an extent they partake of the character of stylized animal heads with distended jaws and lolling tongue. The most common archeological representa-

tion shows the Gorgoneion as human but reminiscent of the raging animal because of the extended tongue and the snarling mouth, and in this representation the animal element is emphasized by the snakes surrounding the head. From this point all sorts of intermediate stages lead to the ideal of antiquity in which the whole face has become completely human."

The themes emphasized by Wundt are first the apotropaic religious nature of the mask and second the human-animal intermixture to achieve various effects, among them fear and terror.

Not too dissimilar is the view of Franz Boas, one of the fathers of modern anthropology: "The use of masks is found among a great number of peoples. The origin of the custom is by no means clear in all cases, but a few typical forms of their use may easily be distinguished. They are intended to deceive spirits as to the identity of the wearer and may thus protect him against attack; or the mask may represent a spirit which is personified by the wearer, who in this way frightens away supernatural enemies. Still other masks are commemorative, the wearer personifying a deceased friend."[3]

Really concrete research exists in just a few instances. One outstanding case is the work of George W. Harley on the secret societies of Liberia. Harley was a physician who spent twenty-three years in northeast Liberia at a time when the secret societies were being successfully repressed by the central government. The masks which had been invariably used by all levels of the (pregovernment) controlling social structure had no further function, and sons of the last possessors sold or gave the artifacts to him. Answers to judicious questions about their use at the time of acquisition were pieced together to make a most perceptive account of the old social structure. A vital part of this structure was the *Poro* secret society. Membership was restricted to initiated males, and masks were vital to the operation of the society. The chief of the high council of elders was also keeper of the great mask known as *Go-ge*. The *mask* had the final approval of decisions of the council. "It had some of the attributes of a living god when worn, and those of a sacred oracle and supreme judge at other times. It was the object of blood sacrifice and prayer." In the old days the sacrifice was human. The Go-ge masks had protuberant eyes and red felt lips and there was black dried blood from sacrifices caked on the face. Such a mask from Harley's collection is shown in Figure 70. Its

Figure 70 (top left). Go-ge mask of black wood from Mano tribe (Liberia). Harley Collection. By permission of Peabody Museum, Harvard University.

Figure 71 (lower left). Go-ge mask of black wood from Mano tribe. "Hears palaver and has sacrifice of sheep" (Liberia). Harley Collection. By permission of Peabody Museum, Harvard University.

Figure 72 (top right). Mask of black wood with reduplicated eyes, from Gio tribe (Liberia). Harley Collection. By permission of Peabody Museum, Harvard University.

Figure 73. Apotropaic shield faces from Sepik River tribes (New Guinea). By permission of Hamburg Museum für Völkerkunde und Vorgeschichte.

apotropaic intent and significance are evident and the importance of the eyes is apparent. A second Liberian mask with similar use is seen in Figure 71. The significance of the eyes and the human-animal complex mentioned by Wundt is seen in a third mask from Harley's collection (Fig. 72). In this example the eyes are emphasized by being doubled.[4]

Similarly the account of Valentine, quoted above, was based on what he was told and what he observed during twelve months spent among the Lalaki of New Britain. He was able to identify twenty-two categories of ceremonial mask personalities. Of these, at least five chase and belabor, or abuse, or bite people as their present allowed function. Valentine does not state what their function might have been in the "old days." However, for nearby New Ireland there is believable evidence that mask personalities, now mildly abusive,

could at one time injure or even kill with impunity.[5]

Even more speculative than the above is the possibility that many apotropaia—faces, masks, Gorgon heads—owe their terrible and repellent properties to their representation of the skull or the severed head of an enemy.

Consider first the central Gorgon myth in which the head of Medusa was presented to Athene, who placed it in the center of her shield. The universality of the aegis (the Athene-Gorgon shield) is shown by the many times in all ages that grotesque faces appear on shields. Three such shields from primitive New Guinea are shown in Figure 73.

The apotropaic nature of the New Guinea shield figure is reinforced by the finding of virtually identical figures that had been used to decorate the gable of a ceremonial house in the same area of New Guinea (Fig.

Figure 74 (left). Apotropaic faces used to decorate gables of Sepik ceremonial house (New Guinea). Note similarity to shield faces of preceding figure. By permission of Field Museum of Natural History, Chicago.

Figure 75 (right). Apotropaic face from Sepik ceremonial dance mask. By permission of Field Museum of Natural History, Chicago.

74). Compare these with a ceremonial dance mask also from the Sepik River, New Guinea (Fig. 75). Once again, the apotropaic nature of the grotesque gable face is intuitively recognized. To reinforce intuition are two illustrations from Reche's early work on the cultures of the Sepik River in northern New Guinea. Figure 76 shows a ceremonial house with a typical gable mask. Below the mask is a row of four embrasures holding human skulls. One is greatly tempted to assume that the apotropaic force of the skulls is wrapped up and packaged in the large, grotesque gable mask.[6]

Lest this be thought an isolated and aberrant phenomenon of the South Pacific, one may refer to Herodotus' description of the Scythian tribe of the Tauri: "When they take prisoners in war they treat them in the following way. The man who has taken a captive cuts off his head, and carrying it home fixes it on a tall pole which he elevates above his house, most commonly over the chimney. The reason that the heads are set up so high, is (it is said) in order that the whole house may be under their protection."[7] This Scythian apotropaic skull is twenty-four centuries and half the earth away from New Guinea in 1908 but the identity of the concepts is inescapable.

A second illustration from New Guinea is that of the head holder which was found inside the ceremonial house of another village on the Sepik River. It was not

Figure 76. Apotropaic gable mask on Sepik ceremonial house. Note skulls in embrasures below mask. By permission of Hamburg Museum für Völkerkunde und Vorgeschichte.

Figure 77. Ceremonial skull holder inside Sepik ceremonial house as photographed by Otto Reche, 1908-1910. By permission of Hamburg Museum für Völkerkunde und Vorgeschichte.

Figure 78. Ceremonial skull holder (minus skulls) found in 1959 in Torembi, New Guinea. By permission of Professor Alfred Bühler.

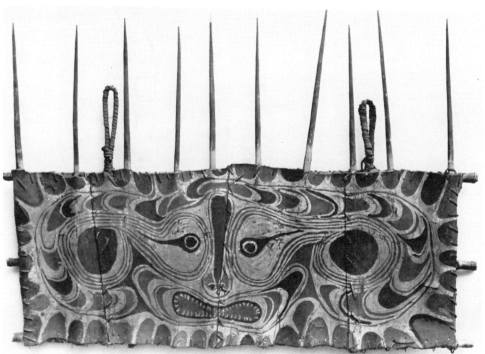

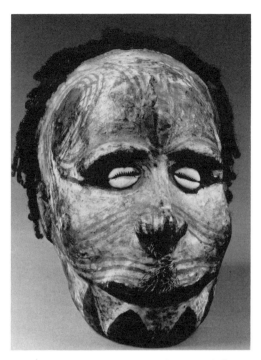

Figure 79. Clay-modeled skull with cowrie shell eyes from Sepik River region. By permission of Staatliche Museen Preussischer Kulturbesitz, Museum für Völkerkunde Berlin, Abteilung Südsee.

Figure 80. Skull with cowrie shell eyes and molded features from ancient Jericho, ca. 7,000-8,000 B.C. Kenyon, *Digging Up Jericho*. By permission of Dame Kathleen Kenyon.

made clear whether this holder was for the heads of ancestors or those of enemies—both were preserved by the Sepik River tribes. However the painted decoration of the head holder is a series of Gorgon-like grotesques (Fig. 77). Curiously, a similar head holder now sans heads appears in the photographic record by René Gardi and Alfred Bühler of the Basel Museum expedition to the Sepik in 1958. The heads were no longer socially acceptable but what appeared to be the holder with its grotesque face had persisted and was photographed (Fig. 78).[8]

One feels compelled to insert here another parallel between primitive New Guinea and an ancient primitive culture. Some of the skulls preserved by the Sepik River tribes were in a manner reconstituted: clay was molded on the skull recreating some semblance of flesh, and in some instances the clay was painted. In an example presented by Reche and in similar skulls reported by the Basel and Berlin expeditions the eyes were replaced by cowrie shells (Fig. 79). Most remarkable is the discovery by Kathleen Kenyon of a set of skulls similarly molded and with similar cowrie shell eyes in the ruins of neolithic Jericho (Fig. 80).[9] This level is datable to 7,000–8,000 B.C.

The Maori of New Zealand were headhunters before British colonization. The Maori are Polynesian and are unlikely to have acquired Melanesian customs from the New Guinea Sepik tribes by direct contact. Nevertheless the similarities are striking. We learn via verbal tradition that the Maori kept the heads of enemies by steaming, smoking, and oiling and put them on posts to be mocked and cursed. When an attack by enemies on a Maori fortress impended, the heads were set up on stakes outside as a set of apotropaic symbols. With the Maori as with the Melanesians of New Guinea the heads of ancestors were also kept for ceremonial occasions. The confusion and ambivalence between the two kinds of heads may be more in the minds of uninformed Western observers than in those of the native practitioners.[10]

Among the Maori, wood carving reached a peak of excellence. How far back the present elegant work goes is unclear, and the story of its origin is incorporated in timeless Maori legend. The artifacts we know are no more than 150 years old. The carving reaches its most elegant in the Maori meetinghouses with their elaborately decorated outer walls. In an excellent example reconstructed in Chicago's Field Museum of Natural History one observes the front wall covered with

Figure 81. Maori meeting house with exterior decoration of faces with flat shell eyes. Note gable mask.
By permission of Field Museum of Natural History, Chicago.

faces containing prominent shell eyes (Fig. 81). The ever-present gable mask (*tekoteko* in Maori) is in this instance less elegant in execution than the wall, but dominant in size and position. One is entitled to ask once more whether the faces on the front wall are not surrogates for the skulls of the Sepik River house and whether the *tekoteko* is not the embodiment of all of the apotropaic forces in the one prominent mask. The finely carved "Tiki" head from New Zealand (Fig. 82) urges confirmation of this idea.

After the original version of this chapter was completed my attention was called to the fascinating essay of Schuster on the potter deity of Aibom. Much of the material in this essay substantiates the hypothesis that one aspect of masks and masking is apotropaic and is connected to the apotropaic force of the human skull. Schuster did his research in the village of Aibom on the Middle Sepik River in northern New Guinea. This gen-

eral area of the Middle Sepik is where some of the material presented earlier in this book and in this chapter originates. In particular one should note the face-pot shown in Figure 62 as an example of an apotropaion. Professor Schuster points out that there are two major types of face-pot made in Aibom—the large sago storage vessels (*au*) and the smaller fire basins (*gugumbe*). Furthermore the gable mask in this village is a *pottery* face. Of the faces depicted there are four standard types for each of the two varieties of pot, and three of the four are similar for the two groups. All are humanoid with animal or fantastic additions. There are a pig face (Fig. 83), an eagle face, and a bush spirit. In addition there is a type similar to a wooden dance mask and a type similar to a human skull with features added modeled in clay (Figs. 79, 84).

Despite the representational similarities, the large sago storage pots were said by native informants to be

Figure 82. "Tiki" (tekoteko) mask from New Zealand, derived from gable mask. By permission of Field Museum of Natural History, Chicago.

Figure 84 Sepik face-pot with humanoid eyes. By permission of Staatliche Museen Preussischer Kulturbesitz, Museum für Völkerkunde Berlin, Abteilung Südsee.

Figure 83. Sepik face-pot with pig face. By permission of Staatliche Museen Preussischer Kulturbesitz, Museum für Völkerkunde Berlin, Abteilung Südsee.

primarily male deity equivalents and the fire basins were said to be female deity equivalents, representing two sisters. The one of particular interest (named Kolimangge) was identical with a dance figure named Yuman Wusmangge which appeared in Aibom during the stay there of the expedition. It is of particular interest that the dance-figure head was a typical clay-modeled skull (cf. Fig. 79).

Thus the connection between the apotropaic face-pot, the gable mask, and the clay-modeled human skull, made by me on theoretical grounds, was made by Professor Schuster from narrative material and observations of his own expedition.

In his discussion of the skull-headed figure Schuster retells a native myth: "The ancestors wanted to show the face of Yuman to the women and children and therefore they made a Tumbuan (a large mask figure). First they tried to make the head out of mud. How-

Figure 85. Sepik face-pot. Compare with examples of Gorgon kylix. By permission of Staatliche Museen Preussischer Kulturbesitz, Museum für Völkerkunde Berlin, Abteilung Südsee.

ever, that was not satisfactory and the head fell apart. Then they tried to make it of wood—but the head broke nevertheless. Then the ancestors killed a very tall enemy by the name of Beoni who belonged to the village of Yangglambit in the bush between Aibom and Korosemeri. For this they made a pit on the bottom of which they stuck spears with the points directed upwards. Beoni ran over the spot, fell in, and died. They cut off his head, cooked it, prepared it with clay, and painted it. Now the Tumbuan had been given the proper head."

Finally Schuster analyzes the entire event of the appearance of Yuman Wusmangge as follows:

From this information it follows, without having to follow this path farther, that Yuman is a cannibalistic entity particularly closely associated with headhunting and human sacrifice. Add to this the information that the figure appeared only if an important personage died or if a new ceremonial house had been completed. This latter happening in modern form was the occasion for its appearance in our case, for the new house of the "Native Society," a native trade association, was to be festively inaugurated. However, it is clearly not the construction as an architectural event that was originally intended but the sacrifice associated with it. A prisoner who had been tied to the tree on the ceremonial mound in front of the ceremonial house was danced around in the night and then killed with spear thrusts the next morning. He was stuffed into a posthole and crushed by the post placed on him. One informant says, as the myth

says too, that in earlier times a man had to be killed to prepare the head. The head of the Yuman figure does not represent the skull of the dead personage even though the death of a villager is the reason for its appearance; the skull is that of a slaughtered enemy. The connection of Yuman Wusmangge to killing in combat appears to be much closer than to natural death, although presumably the two concepts were associated in a fundamental way.[11]

Here we finally have it, then. Although in recent times ambivalence and perhaps shame has confused the function of the preserved enemy head with that of the preserved head of an ancestor, we can be sure that the face on the face-pot, the face on the gable mask, and the face on the dance mask are all the enemy skull apotropaion. It is closely related in feeling to Harley's Go-ge mask, to the Gorgoneion, and to the skull on the tentpole of the Scythian Tauri.

This chapter is not intended to be a review of the extremely complicated subject of masks. The object has been to abstract from the welter of overlapping concepts the truly apotropaic elements and with the help of artifacts from widely separated primitive societies to show probable documentation of the ideas behind them. One finds no Gorgons here (though an observer of the Gorgon kylix might be amazed at Figure 85) any more than one finds living pithecanthropids, but one finds many, many lineal descendants of the concept which underlies Gorgon and primitive mask alike.

6. The Eyes of Argus

When Hans Andersen retold the folktale *The Tinder Box* and wanted to escalate the awesomeness of the dogs guarding the treasure chests, he gave the first dog eyes as large as teacups, the second, eyes as large as mill wheels, and the third, eyes as large as the Round Tower (the Rundetaarn in Copenhagen). This is exactly the approach to the Apotropaic Eye used by the artists of the eye kylix where a pair of eyes occupies the whole side of the vessel. There is another approach to awesomeness and this involves the strength of numbers. There are several instances of this approach in Greek mythology. Consider Cerberus, the dog who guarded the gates of Hell. Vergil described him as three-headed, his neck bristling with snakes. This is escalation by multiplexing eyes (and jaws, of course). An even higher degree of multiplexing is possessed by the legendary Argus. This demigod, fabricator of Jason's ship, the Argo, had his head encircled by a hundred eyes. One pair of eyes at a time was able to sleep while the other ninety-eight kept watch.[1] This is the utimate in Watchbirds, achieved not by enlargement but by multiplexing. Several kinds of ancient and primitive artifacts gain force by this approach. Their apotropaic significance intensified by numbers is highly convincing.

A set of such instances is found at several widely separated spots on the shores of the Pacific. There is even less help and explanation from history and anthropology in these instances than in the subjects previously explored. Once more the artifacts must speak for themselves.

Figure 86 shows a cast-bronze vessel typical of many hundreds that have been found over the centuries at a site in northeast China known as Anyang. These products of highly skilled craftsmen are attributed with reasonable assurance to the Shang Dynasty (1523–1027 B.C.) at a time (1300–1027 B.C.) when Anyang was the dynastic capital. The artisans of the Chou Dynasty (1027–841 B.C.), which destroyed the Shang, took over the bronze manufacture and developed it in their own way. As the Chou Dynasty closed, technology deteriorated and the superb bronze pieces ceased to be produced.

Very curious is the apparent lack of evolution of the technology. As far as anyone can tell, the Shang bronzes sprang into being full-formed and complete. There are no fumbling attempts by unsophisticated aspirants, no midget-sized trial runs. The oldest pieces known to us are in the topmost category artistically and technically. This has led to the theory that the bronzes were the work of craftsmen imported from farther west. The contemporary Luristan bronze workers of western Iran are most frequently mentioned. An alternative possibility is that Chinese archeology is so rudimentary that artifacts revealing the chain of preceding events have not yet been excavated. Indeed before 1950 Anyang was the only known site for Shang and Chou bronzes. Within the next fifteen years some eighty other sites were discovered. There is a hint in the materials of the 1973 show in Paris, presented under the auspices of the People's Republic of China, that the newer excavations have revealed less-finished pieces of very early Shang bronze.[2] However, none of these other sites is as important as Anyang, and none has thrown new light on the question of origins.

The technology is equally curious, for despite the logical assumption that such pieces could have been made only by the "lost wax" process there is solid evidence for another technique. At Anyang clay mold components have been found which are complete design units. This strongly suggests that the bronze pieces were made by "multimold" casting—that the final mold was made of a number of subcomponents each carved in intaglio in the wet clay, fired individually, and luted together to make the final mold. However this may be, the technology is superb. The reason for presenting these details is that if the technology originated outside of China, so might the design elements described below. However, we shall see that the world sites of similar design elements do not coincide with the sites of bronze technology.[3]

The thing that attracts our present interest is the role that the eye plays in the overall decorative scheme of the Shang and Chou bronzes. The majority of representations run to fantastic and not always identifiable animal forms—zoomorphs they may be called. But whatever the animal, the eye is the most prominent feature in every one. This is true both in terms of size relative to other body parts and in terms of height of relief. Figure 87 shows that aspect well. This is not just

Figure 86. Li-Ting, bronze ceremonial food vessel of Shang period. Note prominent eyes of grotesque faces above each leg of the vessel. By permission of Center of Asian Art and Culture, The Avery Brundage Collection, M. H. de Young Museum, San Francisco.

Figure 88 (above). Hu, bronze vessel of late Chou period. Zoomorph decoration has become degraded to a nearly homogeneous pattern, but eyes are still prominent and distinguishable. Courtesy of Freer Gallery of Art, Smithsonian Institution, Washington, D.C.

Figure 87 (left). Kuei, bronze vessel of the Shang period. Zoomorphs are symmetrical on either side of center ridge. In main body of vessel two eyes of a grotesque face stare at the viewer. In base are two zoomorphs with prominent eyes. In upper frieze a small mask appears on center ridge. On either side of the frieze are two zoomorphs with prominent eyes. Courtesy of Freer Gallery of Art, Smithsonian Institution, Washington, D.C.

Figure 89 (left). Ting, bronze vessel of the Shang period. T'ao t'ieh mask, with its prominent Apotropaic Eyes, occupies the entire body of vessel. Courtesy of Freer Gallery of Art, Smithsonian Institution, Washington, D.C.

Figure 90 (right). Fang I, bronze vessel of the Shang period. Mask with Apotropaic Eyes occupies prominent position on body, as does another on lid. Courtesy of Art Institute of Chicago

a selected example, for piece after piece shows the same features. What is more, on many, many pieces there are twenty, a hundred, or even more zoomorphs with bodies not recognizable but with eyes always identifiable (Fig. 88).

A second feature of equal importance to us is the widespread prevalence of the "demon mask" on Shang bronzes. The Chinese designation is *t'ao t'ieh*, whose common meaning is "glutton." However, if this can be legitimately equated with "voracious beast" the term is understandable. Figure 89 shows a typical bronze piece representing such a mask. The vessels of Figures 86, 87, and 90 have prominent masks. Here, too, the eyes are most prominent in size and relief. After our previous consideration of the Gorgoneion and the Gorgon kylix, of the face-pots of Troy and Stentinello, and of the gable masks of the South Pacific, it requires no great leap of imagination to recognize the Shang

demon mask, the *t'ao t'ieh*, as apotropaic. Not surprisingly, others have had the same idea. Waterbury, though not using the term "apotropaic," renames the *t'ao t'ieh* "guardian head"—a near approach.[4]

Chinese documentation is of little use in this matter. There are no direct statements about the significance of the decorations. The first exemplars of Chinese writing anywhere are the brief inscriptions on these very bronzes. Many Shang bronze inscriptions are listed as uninterpretable by Creel, and those which are decipherable are confined to laconic statements. An instance cited by d'Argencé reads, "Uncle [*also used as rank*] made this perfect vessel [here called *Tsun*] to be cherished forever by his descendants." Later Chinese writing is equally uninformative. The writings of the Han period (206 B.C.–A.D. 221) include legends about the vessels but say nothing about form or decoration. The scholars of the Sung period (A.D. 960–1279) were

Figure 91. Li-ho, ceremonial bronze wine vessel of earliest Shang period. Note somewhat primitive apotropaic face in decorative band. By permission of Center of Asian Art and Culture, The Avery Brundage Collection, M. H. de Young Museum, San Francisco.

concerned with the inscriptions. In the middle of the eleventh century a study was made of the vessel forms and of their ritual significance, and an attempt was made to identify the king in whose reign the late bronzes were cast. But there is no continuity of written tradition to give authentic information on design elements. The eleventh-century Sung scholar had no more than the artifacts themselves to work with; he had many fewer pieces than we do; and he was two whole millennia removed in time from the Shang artisans.[5]

Two Shang pieces do much to clarify my outlook on these classic bronzes. The first of these is a *li-ho*

(wine vessel) in the Brundage Collection, identified by Loehr as belonging to the earliest Shang period (Fig. 91).[6] The early date for the piece is based on the identity of its shape with that of many neolithic pottery vessels and on the simplicity of its design. As simple as the design is, it has the same basic elements as all of the other apotropaic vessels we have examined previously. The basic element is a bilaterally symmetrical grotesque face in which the eyes are the most prominent feature. Whatever its other ceremonial implications may be, the vessel is an apotropaic face-pot closely related to those of Troy I and of Stentinello, to the Gorgon kylix, and to the Sepik River pottery. Needless to add, the one most important feature of the apotropaic face is the Apotropaic Eye.

It is easy to understand how the elementary apotropaic face developed into the *t'ao-t'ieh*, but the rest of the subsequent development needs some clarification. The single piece of Shang bronze which does this for me better than any other is the elephant *huo* from the Freer Gallery of the Smithsonian (Fig. 92).

It is clear that the well-represented elephant is rendered very realistically and has his own eyes. But besides this pair of eyes, numerous additional eyes appear all over his exterior. This says to me that the Shang artist knew that the Apotropaic Eye was the key feature of his ritual bronze vessel—whether he knew why this is so is immaterial. He did not choose, as did the Gorgon kylix potters, to make the largest pair of eyes the vessel could accommodate. He chose another route—the multiplication of eyes—on the basis that if one pair of Apotropaic Eyes is good, many pairs are better. This, it seems to me, is the key to one aspect of the design of the Shang bronze vessels. The basic animal represented, if this animal can be identified positively, does have significance of its own, but the essential common feature of all the vessels is the replicated Apotropaic Eye. Let us recall that there has been a hint of strength through multiplexing in some of the material reviewed in an earlier chapter. The Eye of Horus was not only quadruple (Fig. 28) but in one of Petrie's finds was repeated twenty times. The eye beads and eye amulets are similarly multiplied. The ultimate result of this process occurs in some of the Chou pieces where the body of the dragon or tiger or unidentifiable animal has been reduced to a low-relief geometrical pattern that decorates a rectangular space. However the eyes are prominent to the last; even though their apotropaic potency is probably long forgotten, they

Figure 92. Huo, ceremonial bronze of Shang period in form of elephant. Note that zoomorphs covering elephant have Apotropaic Eyes, most of them larger than elephant's own. By permission of Freer Gallery of Art, Smithsonian Institution, Washington, D.C.

Figure 93. Pen hu, bronze jar of "Warring States" period, 481-221 B.C. Zoomorphs are completely stylized and enclosed in rectangular panels. Courtesy of Art Institute of Chicago.

Figure 94 (below). One panel of pen hu in Fig. 93. Apotropaic Eyes of zoomorphs still detectable by relatively large size, elevation, and central pupil. Courtesy of Art Institute of Chicago.

Figure 95. Blanket of Northwest Coast Indian origin (Tlingit, Koluschan stock). Note bilateral symmetry, mask above, and multiple Apotropaic Eyes. By permission of Field Museum of Natural History, Chicago.

stand in high relief and are repeated time after time in each of the rectangles (Figs. 93, 94).

The other side of the north Pacific holds an art form that is just as striking, just as unusual, and to my mind based on the same principle as the Shang bronzes. This is the two-dimensional art of the Northwest Coast Indians—in particular, the tribes of the southern panhandle of Alaska and the coat of British Columbia as far south as the northern end of Vancouver Island. Consider the Chilkat blanket shown in Figure 95, which epitomizes most of the characteristic elements of interest to us. The prominence (here relative size only—there is no third dimension) and the multiplication of eyes is immediately apparent. Such designs are seen not only woven into blankets, but carved into elegant wooden chests, and painted on ceremonial hats.

Once again, existing written records are of no use to us. The first European contact with the Northwest Coast Indian tribes was made by the Russian expedition of Bering in 1741. The first dated artifacts were collected by Captain James Cook on his third voyage in 1778. A wooden bowl collected by this expedition and possessing one pair of supernumerary eyes is now in the British Museum. None of the written records of these or subsequent expeditions tell us "why the eye."[7]

In the late nineteenth and early twentieth century the Northwest Coast culture attracted the attention of professional anthropologists beginning with Franz Boas. He published an account of the indigenous art in 1897, which was later revised for his 1927 book *Primitive Art*. It is generally agreed that the animal representations are totemic and in the three-dimensional art the individual animals are easily recognized. This is true of spoon handles, house posts, dance masks, and the carved portions of war helmets and ceremonial hats.[8]

Figure 96. Carved coffin of cedar (Bella Bella, British Columbia). Iconographic eye elements of the blanket in Fig. 95 persist here. In addition note the eye-hand motif. By permission of Field Museum of Natural History, Chicago.

However, in the two-dimensional art—the woven blankets, painted house fronts, painted dance costumes, painted portion of hats, and in the carved chests which are two-dimensional in spirit—one finds abstraction of a different and greater order of magnitude. For an extended discussion of levels of abstraction labeled as *configurative, expansive,* and *distributive* see Holm.[9] The degree of abstraction is such that even the native artist informants used by the American Museum on its expeditions gave contradictory interpretations of the animals represented. Boas cites the interpretation of the figures on a number of Chilkat blankets in the version of Lieutenant Emmons and in the version of J. R. Swanton. The first of four blankets was described as a bear with young in the Emmons report (E) and as a sea grizzly bear in the Swanton report (S). Blanket two is a female wolf with young in E, a young raven in S. Blanket three is a bear sitting up according to E, a halibut according to S. Blanket four is a diving whale in the account of E, a wolf with young in the account of S. In the same vein the best carver and painter among the Haida, Charles Edensaw, could not identify the animal represented by body parts on a set of the characteristic gambling sticks when asked by Boas in 1897.[10]

Thus we find ourselves in a familiar situation. There is no written tradition on Northwest Coast Indian art and the oral tradition is so faulty that native artists at the turn of the century could not even identify the animals in the two-dimensional art forms, much less give the reasons behind the symbolism. Once more we are left with the artifacts themselves, along with whatever conjectures have been made about them by art historians and anthropologists. Once more the multiplicity and prominence of eyes as seen in the blanket in Figure 95 or the chest in Figure 96 are most impressive.

This finding could not fail to excite comment in the past, and a number of the comments are worth examining. There is the opinion of Adam, who correctly observes that many of the supererogatory eyes we have been discussing are located at limb joints in the animals represented. These, he says, are not eyes at all but "X ray views" of the joints. "These eye ornaments drawn on claws often look like birds' heads. Sometimes they are even filled in with faces, which have no significance, but are purely decorative additions." I find this view unacceptable precisely because of the existence of the face. The face exists just because the original designer recognized the eyes as eyes and constructed a face to go with them. Furthermore, although many of the supernumerary eyes have been placed at joint locations, by no means all of them are found there. Moreover, in the case of the hand-eye structures which are common in Northwest Coast art (Fig. 19) the single eye present in the palm has to represent the

Figure 97. House in Skidgate, Queen Charlotte Islands. All apotropaic elements of Figs. 95 and 96 are present. Mask is especially prominent. By permission of Field Museum of Natural History, Chicago.

more than fifteen articulations of carpal and metacarpal bones (if the hand is human). This is too excessive a disproportion to be credible.[11]

An exhaustive treatment of the joint-marks was made by Schuster, who gathered pictorial data from the entire Pacific area. Schuster agreed that the marks occur predominantly at joints. However, on the basis of a mass of evidence amid which the faces figured strongly, he concluded that the joint-marks are abbreviated eyes which may in turn be abbreviated faces. An outstanding example of fully expressed faces appears in Figure 97. Schuster reproduced several drawings of tattoos and scarifications of varying degrees of recognizability as eye and face symbols. Highly significant is the account of Bogoras repeated by Schuster, that among the Chukchee, a maritime tribe of the Kamchatka region of Siberia, the tattoo is now a hunting tally but formerly was a homicide tally. If one is dealing with abbreviated skulls in the "joint-marks" that are really eyes, then apotropaic force and force by multiplexing are accomplished at one time.[12]

Others have written detailed description and analysis of the forms and shapes used and have purposely abstained from interpreting the symbolism. This is particularly true of Boas and Holm, and strictly on the basis of data available is entirely justified.

The most fascinating conjectures about Northwest Coast art are those dealing with the similarities between these abstractions and those of the Shang bronze artists. The first observation of similarity was made by Creel in 1935 and echoed by Adam in 1936, by Hentze in 1937. Of the two points made by Creel, the first was that only in Shang art and Northwest Coast art does one come across the frontal presentation of an animal as if it were split from behind and hinged out on the midnasal line (Figs. 87 and 95, for example). This split presentation of the Northwest Coast art was discussed in detail by Boas in 1927.[13]

The second point is stated by Creel as follows: "The Northwest Coast Indians also make a great deal of use of extra heads, beaks and eyes added on the plain surfaces of larger animals, in a way reminiscent of, but not identical with the Shang practice. The many isolated eyes used by the Northwest Coast designers recall most forcibly their similar use in Shang art, and cause one to wonder if there was some magical reason for this which was possessed by both peoples." My answer to this speculation is that there is indeed a magical reason—the eyes of the Chinese pieces and of the Northwest Indian designs are apotropaic and have been emphasized by multiplexing.

Additional force is added to this hypothesis by examination of artifacts originating from a third area as far from the Northwest Coast sites as these are from North China. I refer to the superbly figured pottery of

Figure 98. Evolution of multiplex eyes and persistence of apotropaic mask in feline figures decorating Peruvian pottery (Juan Pablo region, Peru). After Sawyer, "Paracas and Nazca Iconography." Reproduced by permission of Mr. Sawyer.

Figure 99. Falcon bottle (Juan Pablo region, Peru). Note stylized eyes at very front. Courtesy of the Art Institute of Chicago.

prehistoric Peru, which once more lacks any contemporary documentation. Many face-pots were made in Peru, and these seem to me to be truly apotropaic faces—not to be confused with human and animal effigy-pots whose significance need not be directly apotropaic. Of all the Peruvian face-pots the incised ware from the south coast includes some of the most impressive examples (Figs. 59, 60). A stylized fanged feline face is a popular motif (Fig. 59). This head is frequently seen alone without representation of a body. It has the feral characteristics specified by Wundt as conveying apotropaic properties. Indeed, the invariably bared fangs and the lolling tongue sometimes depicted are typical Gorgon attributes.

Most impressive of all, however, is an analysis of the evolution of the feline figure on Peruvian pottery from the Juan Pablo region done by Alan Sawyer. Using four pieces of pottery of successively later manufacture, Sawyer showed increased stylization and an increase in number of ectopic eyes from one to three (with retention of the original two) (Fig. 98). Additional emphasis on this point appears in Juan Pablo pottery whose major decorative theme is an incised stylized falcon. As Sawyer remarks, the tail design begins with "simple panels of Chavinoid eye motifs." Once again these elements are multiplexed in later work. In such a Juan Pablo bottle from the middle period in the collection of the Art Institute of Chicago (Fig. 99) the tail is composed of the same multiple eye motifs seen in the last feline figure of Sawyer (Fig. 98, bottom).[14] This is as clear a statement as one could wish of the apotropaic character of the original figure, of the essential nature of the eyes in maintaining that character, and of the increase in apotropaic force gained by multiplexing the eyes even while stylizing the other representational elements. I feel it is quite justifiable to assume that a parallel series could be constructed in Shang bronzes and in Chilkat and Haida art if the examples were as numerous and covered as great a time period as in the Juan Pablo pottery.

Whatever the dynamic behind such a totally world-pervading element as the Ojo de Dios, to be discussed in chapter 7, it seems reasonable that the multiplex evolution of the eyes in the Juan pablo pottery was a purely local affair. The series of stylistic change seems to follow a natural evolution that occurred on the original locale, rather than exhibiting a revolutionary break that one might expect to see if a whole new idea had been imported from abroad.

The larger question of cultural diffusion hinted at

by Creel—that is, whether the design ideas actually traveled from the China of the tenth century B.C. to fifth- to nineteenth-century America to be reflected in Chilkat and Haida art—is neither answerable nor relevant to our present inquiry. Nevertheless there are two petty items that nudge one's wish to speculate. One of these is the equation made by Collins between the composite masklike carvings of the Ipiutak Eskimos at Point Hope, Alaska, and the carvings found in Shang graves near Anyang. The importance of this equation, if it be a correct one, is that it places a Shang motif of an entirely different sort in Alaska. The fact that Hsio-Yen Shih who reported the Shang masks called them apotropaic and the fact that Collins compared the high-relief eyes of the Eskimo ivories with the *t'ao t'ieh* masks of the Shang bronzes, is fascinating because it shows the power with which these ancient artifacts suggests to moderns an interpretation that fits in with my own syntheses.[15]

The second petty item is the appearance of the front of a decorated spruce-root clan hat of the Kwakiutl. This object from British Columbia now in the Field Museum contains at its front a decoration that looks for all the world like a *t'ao t'ieh* mask (Fig. 100).

However, for the purposes of our discussion it makes not the slightest difference whether the Multiplex Eye of the Shang and Chou bronzes migrated across the Bering Strait from China, or whether the lost antecedents of Northwest Coast art showed the same evolution from simple to multiplex which appears to be demonstrable for China and is demonstrated for Peru. It seems to me that the symbolism of the Chilkat blankets and the Haida chests is precisely comparable to that of the Freer Gallery elephant and the Juan Pablo cat, where the designer, fascinated by the apotropaic power of the eye, multiplied that eye over the body of an animal that already had two good eyes of its own.

Figure 100. Clan hat of spruce roots from Kwakiutl tribe (British Columbia). By permission of Field Museum of Natural History, Chicago.

7. The Ojo de Dios

It is strange enough that the subject matter of this chapter should be labeled "Eye of God" in Spanish. Add to that its popularity in the counterculture, its origin in a still-surviving tribe, and its worldwide dissemination at an unknown period in the past, and you have the makings of a confusing and amazing story. I shall try to make that story understandable as far as available facts allow.

One of the component ideas of the Watchbird concept complex referred to in chapter 1 is the notion that the gods are watching the actions of men. An improbable physical locus for this concept, and a place where it has been concretized in a symbol, is a remote spot in the southern Sierra Madre Occidental of Mexico. This is the sparsely inhabited interior of the state of Nayarit where the Huichol tribe has dwelt since before the white man came. Here we are in a bit of luck with documentation. The area is cut off from the rest of Mexico by steep mountains and deep canyons carved by rivers that are impassible in the rainy season. There was no gold and virtually no easily arable land, so even the nominal conquest of the area waited until 1722—two hundred years after the rest of Mexico came under Spanish rule. Add to this a beautifully resilient culture which assimilated Christian features to itself but was never supplanted by Christianity and you have an anthropological fossil extremely well preserved. It is our additional good fortune that a durable and perceptive anthropologist visited the Huichols from 1895 to 1898. Carl Lumholtz of the American Museum asked some of the right questions for our purposes and got straightforward answers which he published in detail.[1] Even today despite the inroads of the twentieth century (which inroads include American anthropologists) the Huichols preserve their ancient traditions. They still make an annual pilgrimage of several hundred miles to northwest San Luis Potosi to collect the peyote which plays a central role in their ritual. One intriguing account of such a pilgrimage is given by Furst and another comes from his associate Meyerhof.[2]

Whether the effect of the peyote hallucinogen on color perception plays a major part or not, the Huichols created (and still create) marvelous plaques of colored wools and bowls lined with colored stones or seeds. Equally important, they thread colored wools on a pair of sticks tied at right angles to form a cross. The resulting lozenge-shaped objects composed of concentric rows of various colors were called *sikuli* in the Indian dialect, or *eyes*. Lumholtz was told that the eyes of the gods looked out through the center spot, viewing the deeds of men. The consistency and openness of the Huichols is attested to by the fact that Zingg in his 1938 report confirmed this information exactly. He says: "A native verified for me Lumholtz' statement that 'the prayer expressed by this symbolic object is that the eye of the god may rest upon the supplicant.' "[3] Among the Huichols the *sikuli* were always hung from ceremonial arrows and there was a connection between the design of the shields of the ancient tribes and the design of the lozenge. Each of the color patterns is said to have had a special significance.

It seems logical to assume that the Ojo de Dios was an integral part of prehistoric culture in much or all of Mesoamerica. It also seems reasonable to think that it survived intact among the Huichols from pre-Columbian times. Apparently it radiated south from the Sierra Madre Occidental to southern Mexico and to Mexico City in recent times and the California counterculture imported it from there. Throughout Latin America the object is universally known as Ojo de Dios (= Eye of God), the Spanish equivalent of the Huichol term. It is looked on now as an amulet against the Evil Eye. This is a curious fusion of the Indian tradition with that of the Spanish Mediterranean. Figures 101 to 104 show examples from the midcontinent area where the Ojo de Dios prevails.

That the Ojo de Dios should exist as a phenomenon narrowly disseminated from a mountain tribe in Mexico was entirely believable. If such a tribe, given to the use of mescaline, wanted to call a rhombus made of yarn an eye, that was certainly their affair. The thing I found astounding was that this same device—the Ojo de Dios—is a worldwide phenomenon, and depiction of the eye as a rhombus is much more general than its appearance in Mesoamerica. When the Ojo de Dios appears elsewhere it is known to anthropologists as the thread-cross or Fadenkreuz. The subject has had considerable attention from professionals in the field. Through the notable reviews of Foy and Lindblom one finds that the thread-cross itself or logical variants of it exist among primitive tribes throughout the world.[4]

Figure 101. Ojo de Dios (Bolivia). A good example showing basic structure.

Figure 103. Ojo de Dios (Mexico). Cruciform structure.

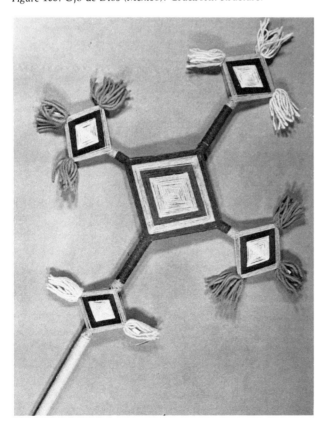

Figure 102. Ojo de Dios (Mexico). Similarly basic structure, but with mirror added at center.

Figure 104. Ojo de Dios (Mexico). Fanciful new form for tourist consumption.

One must add parenthetically that there exist also, in much smaller numbers, devices wound on three or even four crossed sticks instead of two. These result in hexagonal or octagonal thread figures designated by the general term *Fadenstern* or thread-star. They appear to be an afterthought or an elaboration of the thread-cross, being found in the same general anthropological situations. They are, altogether, less important than the thread-cross, which appears to be the basic device. The thread-cross has been found on every continent and in Oceania. Even in northern Europe comparable relics exist associated with obviously pagan observances. Even more striking is the fact that although in some primitive tribes these devices are simply carried in ceremonial dances, their past use forgotten, in many, many locations the design is still considered an amulet with a definite role in warding off evil, in restricting spirits of the dead to their graves, in detecting witches, or in furthering fertility of animals and crops.

Let us examine the world occurrence of the Ojo de Dios in some detail. An immediate point of focus is South America, for here there is archeological evidence for the pre-Columbian existence of this artifact. A detailed report is given by Lothrop and Mahler of "yarn-wrapped reeds" in a pit-grave at Zapallan in the central coast area of Peru. Some of these are wrapped in a diamond pattern. With them are associated thread-crosses having the same geographical distribution as the yarn-wrapped reeds—some 150 miles of Peruvian coast between the Huara and the Rimac rivers. The Ojo de Dios is thought to be older than the yarn-wrapped reeds because a variant has been found in graves of the Proto-Lima period, dated before A.D. 500. Even more suggestive is the description by Lumholtz of a Peruvian mummy from Ancon on which Ojos de Dios serve as eyes for the customary false head of the outer case, and the diamond-shaped devices were precisely placed so that the acute angles corresponded to the corners of the eyes. Similar but presumably not identical pieces were illustrated by Reiss and Stübel and were described as also coming from Ancon in the central coast area. Finally an 1838 report describes a gilt thread Ojo de Dios in a prehistoric burial in Colombia.[5]

Thus in the case of the Huichols there is a tradition that puts the Ojo de Dios in prehistory. In the case of the central Peruvian coast and Colombia there are archeological finds that place it there firmly. Moreover,

two of these finds equate the Peruvian construction with the eye unequivocally. There is no identifiable cultural bridge in South America like that of the Huichols in Mexico to explain how numerous primitive tribes in South America have come to use the Ojo de Dios today. Nevertheless, it is reasonable to postulate such a temporal bridge, for no fewer than nineteen modern occurrences have been documented by anthropologists. Most of the evidence comes from the compendium of Foy and the addendum of Lindblom. The world incidence of the thread-cross is shown in Appendix B and the numerous South American sites are evident.

Despite the "eye" nomenclature of the Huichol Indians and despite the mummy burial with the Ojo de Dios on its eyes one still might view with considerable scepticism the notion that the concentric rhombus was a universal symbol of the eye. There is virtually nothing in modern Western symbolism to bear out this idea. I myself was certainly sceptical until in other contexts I came across a number of lozenge-shaped eyes that were unmistakably eyes. Some of the eyes on the face-pots of Troy I as shown by Blegen were lozenge-shaped (Fig. 57). These are dated at 3000–2500 B.C. The eyes on the Stentinello pottery of Sicily mentioned in chapter 4 are definitely rhomboid and are unquestionably eyes (Fig. 58). Moreover, the rhomboid eye is a not uncommon feature of the cylinder seals of the Middle East in the middle of the second millennium B.C.[6] Such an eye appears in a Mittanian cylinder of that era (Fig. 34). Thus one is brought squarely against the fact that not only does the Ojo de Dios rhombus represent a worldwide design, not only did it originate in prehistory, but it appeared in places as far apart in time and space as Sicily in the third millennium B.C., Asia Minor in the mid-second millennium, and South America at the end of the second millennium. In each of these widely separated locales the symbol was unmistakably an eye symbol.

Only one modern instance of the equation of the thread-cross rhombus to an eye is known to me. This occurs in an 1885 report of Emil Riebeck who brought a thread-cross back to the Berlin Museum for Ethnology from his 1882 trip to the Chittagong Mountains (now part of Bangladesh). Riebeck described the object as a "talisman which is erected before the village by the Lushai tribe as a protection against disease. It is an eye-like amulet made of a little bamboo cross by winding black, red and white cotton threads around it."[7] In other modern accounts, although there are many references to the amuletic significance of the thread-cross, it is not endowed with eyelike properties.

Early on when we discussed the Ojo de Dios among the Huichols we were dealing with a North American locale. Besides the Huichols, a neighboring tribe (the Cora) and a Northwest Mexico tribe (the Tarahumara) are described by Lumholtz as making thread-crosses. Other examples have been collected from the Yuma, Zuni, and Hopi tribes. There is even one description of a thread-cross dance ornament worn on the head by women of the Northwest Coast Indians on Vancouver Island. Thus, although the Ojo de Dios exists in North America and although it persists through the durable Huichols, it has not been widely disseminated until recent years. Tourists and counterculturists in the last decade have spread it through the United States from coast to coast, but it is doubtful whether either the ocular or amuletic significance is appreciated.

The thread-cross has been found in Africa both north and south of the Sahara, but in all cases it seems concentrated near the three coasts.

The 1967 review of Kauffmann on the thread-cross in Africa, incorporating and enlarging upon the earlier writings of Foy and Lindblom, is the most complete to date. Thirty-seven different instances are reported, but very little information is presented on their significance. In only a few instances is apotropaic influence stated or implied and in no case is any mention made of eye symbolism.[8]

An African thread-cross now in the Swedish Ethnographic Museum is unusual in that the standard is iron although the threads are colored cotton (Fig. 105). It comes from the Cameroun Mountain and from a period before the German occupation of the Cameroons, but nothing is known of its function or significance.

Two other African items come from Angola (Fig. 106). In both of these the design is made of colored straw, a not uncommon finding in African "thread-crosses" (more than half of Kauffmann's thirty-seven items are of straw or bark or leather rather than thread). The two items in Figure 106 were used as hair ornaments by both men and women in ceremonial dances in the Mubundu and Ngangela tribes.

In another part of Africa there is documentation for use of a two-dimensional representation of the thread-cross rather than the object itself as an apotropaion. On the reinforcing straps of the tents of Bedouins in

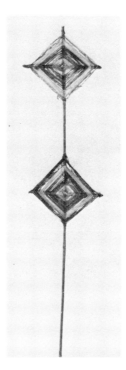

Figure 105. Thread-cross (Mt. Cameroun or South Nigeria). Statens Etnografiska Museet, Stockholm. Courtesy of Prof. G. Lindblom.

Figure 106 (below). Thread-crosses used as hair ornaments (Angola). Statens Etnografiska Museet, Stockholm. Courtesy of Prof. Lindblom.

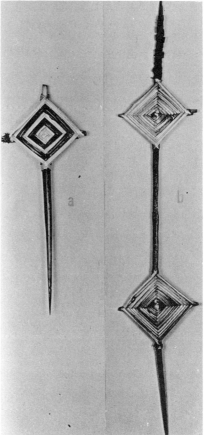

Figure 107. "Unruh" (Tirol). From W. Foy, "Fadenstern und Fadenkreuz," *Ethnologica* 2 (1913).

Figure 108. Thread-cross with feathers interwoven in thread pattern (Aranda tribe, central Australia). By permission of Basel Museum of Anthropology.

central Algeria there are numerous embroidered decorations. In at least two instances lozenge shapes which unmistakably resemble the thread-cross are said to avert the Evil Eye.[9]

It is somewhat surprising that there are documented instances of thread-crosses (and straw- or rush-crosses) found in Europe. It is less surprising that the gloss of Western civilization has suppressed any major consciousness of the significance of these constructs. There are accounts, for example, of straw- or rush-crosses in eight of the thirty-two counties of Ireland. They are associated with the harvest or Saint Brigid's Day. Andrews, the informant on Ireland, is convinced that the practice is not only pre-Christian but even pre-Celtic. Similar structures made of Saint-John's-wort are common in the department of Landes in France and are said to "prevent the entrance of evil spirits" into peasant cottages.[10]

Similar structures have been identified in Scandinavia and the Baltic states. They were used on maypoles in Finland and displayed on Christmas Eve in Sweden. The Swedish examples were traditionally made of mountain ash and called "Yulrönn" (*rönn* = *rowan* = *mountain ash*). In Estonia they were used at Christmas, New Years, and on other festive occasions such as weddings.[11]

Another European variant of the thread-cross is the general category of "Unruh." This term (= *unrest*) was applied to the pendulum of a clock or the balance wheel of a watch. In the case of our object (Fig. 107) we are talking about a hanging ornament which more nearly than anything else resembles the "mobile" structures popularized by the modern artist Alexander Calder. However, the components of our *Unruh* are straw models of the thread-cross and in the particular one shown here there is a crude, centrally hung dove symbolizing the Holy Ghost. The *Unruh* is found in Bavaria, in the Tirol, in Holstein, in Frisia, and in Denmark and Sweden. It hangs in the window, over the dining table, as a votive offering. In Bavaria it is said to stop moving in the presence of a witch.

Perhaps the most unusual European manifestation of the thread-cross is the enormous lozenge-shaped headdress worn in the Salzburg region and known as "Tafelperchten." This is thought to have been used in an ancient fertility ceremony. But once more in these forms of thread-cross we are dealing with a pre-Christian phenomenon whose origins, not surprisingly, are completely beclouded.

In Oceania (including Australia) no fewer than thirty-two thread-cross or thread-star sites had been identified by Foy as early as 1913. The range is wide, with highest concentrations in Australia and the New Guinea area. One feels that this is merely a sampling and by no means exhaustive. As in Africa, one is dealing largely with a decorative item used in ritual dances without knowledge or conveyance of knowledge of any apotropaic significance. Figure 108 comes from the Aranda tribe living in the Musgrave Ranges of central Australia. It is unmistakably a thread-cross and was used in the harvest ceremony. The thread-crosses in Figure 109 are also Australian. The larger pair come from Sunday Island in King's Sound and the smallest one is from the Mangala tribe, in the Kimberleys, northwest Australia.

In Asia the chief concentration of our thread-cross = Eye of God appears to be in the Indochina peninsula and on up into Tibet. The remotest point of origin on our list is Inner Mongolia (Fig. 110).

Unlike Africa and Oceania, these areas have a fairly extensive and flourishing priesthood which, at least in Tibet, is strongly Buddhist in derivation and has in many tribal locations taken over the thread-cross from an earlier pagan cult. Again unlike Africa and Oceania, these areas have a tradition in which the use of the device is clearly apotropaic although the application is not uniform in every locale.

The person most interested in the thread-cross in Indochina is Hans Kauffmann. His extensive article is highly recommended though he scorns to make any connection with the eye (p. 51).[12] Kauffmann describes usage of the thread-cross in sixteen separate locales among the Naga hill tribes of Assam as "an integral component of the ceremonies surrounding death." With local variations thread-crosses are used to outfit the grave platform or grave-shelter of the newly deceased. The legend associated with the usage varies. "The thread-cross prevents the spirit of the deceased from returning to his home and causing mischief there." Or, "The thread-cross is needed by the deceased to present to the 'tester of souls' (a Rhadamanthus equivalent) to allow the soul of the deceased to pass on its journey."

In both of these ideas the concept of the thread-cross as "ghost catcher" or as "spirit trap" begins to appear. This is even clearer in the usage of the thread-cross among the Lushai tribes of the Chittagong hills (Bangladesh-India-Burma). Here it is commonly used

Figure 109. Thread-crosses from Sunday Island and (smallest one) from Mangala tribe, Kimberleys, northwestern Australia. Statens Etnografiska Museet, Stockholm. By permission of Prof. G. Lindblom.

Figure 110. Thread-cross (Inner Mongolia). Statens Etnografiska Museet, Stockholm. By permission of Prof. G. Lindblom.

Figure 111 (top left). Thread-cross ceremony (Tibet). Winding five colored threads on frame of thread-cross. Photos on this page from Stephan Beyer, *The Cult of Tara*. Courtesy of Prof. Beyer. Originally published by the University of California Press; reprinted by permission of The Regents of the University of California.

Figure 112 (top right). Portrait complete with house, servants, livestock, and property.

Figure 113 (lower left). Planting shrubbery on surrounding mountains.

Figure 114 (lower right). Entire structure tied around outside with thread and set on altar facing assembly.

in the ceremony to drive out illness, serving as part of the symbolic sacrifice to expel the evil spirits causing disease.

Most elaborate of all is the role of the thread-cross in Tibet. It seems clear that when Buddhism spread from India to Tibet in the seventh century a primitive animistic religion called Bon was already being practiced there. The comparisons between the animistic Bon, concerned with the placation of demons, and the spiritual Buddhism read for all the world like the comparisons between the chthonic religion of the Greeks and the newer cult of the Olympian deities (see chapter 4). Early Buddhist writings are the source for the information that the thread-cross was a well-established part of the Bon ritual and that it played a role in repelling the demons—that is, that it was an apotropaion.[13]

To put things as simply as possible, there occurred in Tibet a synthesis of Bon elements and Buddhist elements known today as Lamaism. The remoteness and relative inaccessibility of Tibet precluded serious study of this synthesis until well into the twentieth century, but relatively recently a number of reports on the subject have been generated by serious students.[14] While space does not allow an adequate summary of the forty pages devoted to the thread-cross ritual of Tara by Dr. Beyer, he has allowed us to reproduce in Figures 111–14 a set of photographs from which one can get a visual impression of the elaborateness of the physical arrangements. In the ceremony as performed for Dr. Beyer the thread-cross structure being built in Figure 111 is placed on an elaborate four-tiered platform made of earth or barley flour mixed with water ("Mount Meru") and surmounted by a "mansion" made of the same material. The mansion is fronted by a portrait said to represent the person for whom the ritual is performed and the "evil spirits will be coerced into accepting it [the figure] as a scapegoat for his person." The remaining substitutes represent the household, property, and possessions of the threatened person; these are molded of dough. A close-up of the platform, mansion, portrait, and subsidiary figures is shown in Figure 112 and the structure with thread-crosses in place is seen in Figure 113. The complete ceremonial table fronted with a hundred butter lamps is seen in Figure 114.

Beyer, agreeing with Lessing and Nebesky-Wojkowitz, suggests that the thread-cross represents a complex of symbolisms containing three main components. These are: (1) Thread-cross as demon trap. This is connected with the resemblance of the device to a spider web that by a slight poetic extension can catch spirits. (2) Thread-cross (as well as the portrait it surmounts in the specific Tara ceremony) as substitute, or scapegoat, for the person threatened by the spirits. (3) Thread-cross as attached to a universe *in parvo*, with all essential elements in the small world that correspond to the large one. Hence it is attractive to the threatening spirits in its verisimilitude. Since the entire apparatus is destroyed at the completion of the ceremony—by fire, by being left in a lonely place, or by being thrown over a cliff—the trapped spirits are destroyed with it and its purpose has been fulfilled.[15]

In Asia, then, we find once more a rather elaborate set of constructs to explain the function of the thread-cross. That function is patently apotropaic, although it is not explained in a way that corresponds to the Watchbird concept of the Huichols of Mexico with the thread-cross symbolizing the eye. On the other hand with the origin of the Asiatic thread-cross in a prehistoric cult that spread over much of central Asia, a cult that left no written record, who can say what was or was not the original motivating symbolism?[16] We must be satisfied to conclude that the Ojo de Dios = Thread-Cross is a nearly universal apotropaion. In the western hemisphere, at least, it is the symbol of an Apotropaic Eye.

8. The Eye of Providence

On the reverse of the great seal of the United States an eye in a triangle surrounded by rays is a prominent feature of the design (Fig. 115). The reverse of the seal has never been used for state purposes but it may be seen on the back of the one-dollar bill. What is the significance of this eye?

The committee that produced the design for the seal was appointed after dinner on July 4, 1776, and consisted of Benjamin Franklin, John Adams, and Thomas Jefferson. In their report to Congress the committee described an original version of the seal with the eye on the obverse, calling it the *Eye of Providence.* No more information is given nor was any needed in the last quarter of the eighteenth century. The symbol was well known then, for it had appeared on coins and in baroque altar decoration and it had been adopted by Freemasonry. It is probably from this last source that it reached our seal, for Franklin had been a high-ranking Masonic official for more than forty years.[1]

However, if one looks for an account of the origin of the symbol or the rationale behind it one finds very little information indeed. Descriptions of its occurrence abound in the German literature under *Auge Gottes,* but there are no accompanying descriptions of significance or background. All of the following is based on documented iconography for which there is no accompanying text but for which the conclusions appear to be inevitable nevertheless.

From our position in the twentieth century it seems perfectly obvious that the triangle symbolizes the Trinity of Christian theology, and indeed it must. However, there was no iconographic tradition for this in the early seventeenth century when the symbol arose, for by a curious quirk the triangle was very rare in Christian symbolism through the entire Middle Ages. The reason for this is that it had been adopted by the Manichaeans under Bishop Faustus, and in his efforts to stamp out Manichaean heresy Saint Augustine forbade the use of the triangle in all applications.[2]

Thus the triangle did not return to Western symbolism via religious art but through the quasi-religious mysticism of alchemy, astronomy, Cabala, Rosicrucianism, and, finally, Freemasonry. The point of return lies in the coinage of the seventeenth and eighteenth centuries. On a medal of Charles II struck in 1660 and on another of William II struck in 1690, one

finds the eye in triangle radiate very much as it appears on the great seal. This was reproduced on hundreds of coin dies engraved in the following century, especially in the cities of Germany.[3] Figure 116 shows a typical example.

Although the term *alchemical* has been used earlier as a description of the nature of several of the texts where the triangle appears, the nature of alchemy has not been discussed, nor is this a simple thing to do. Alchemy must be considered as a philosophical system based on and elaborated from the elementary chemistry known in the Middle Ages. Some elementary chemical techniques such as the smelting of metals were known in dynastic Egypt, ancient Mesopotamia and ancient China. The Greek philosophical attempts to show that the world is made up of four elements had a parallel in China where five elements were posited. However foggy its origins, alchemy is a creature of the Middle Ages. Its ancient components were preserved by the medieval Arab alchemists, and with an accretion of new material from this source it entered Europe via Spain in Latin translation. The avowed objective of alchemy was creation of the philosophers' stone. This was thought to be not only a transmuting agent that converted base metals into gold, but the key to health and long life. Understandably, anyone working toward such a power-conferring goal would shroud his work in secrecy. When principles and discoveries were to be communicated, this was done by allegory and symbols. Thus, in addition to accumulating a certain body of knowledge about elementary chemistry, alchemy became a treasure house of symbolism. The psychiatrist Jung devoted an entire book to psychiatry and alchemy. The unorthodox artist Max Ernst drew heavily upon alchemical symbolism.[4]

The triangle was not lacking among alchemical symbols as can be seen in the printed works that appeared in the sixteenth and seventeenth centuries. It should be appreciated that the material finally disclosed in these books represents the accumulated body of alchemical thought, not just the ideas of the often anonymous author at the date of publication. Consider three figures that appeared in the *Janitor Pansophus,* one of the components of the *Musaeum Hermeticum,* an alchemical compendium of 1678 (illustrations not in the 1625 edition) (Figs. 117–19). In

Figure 115. Great seal of the United States of America (reverse)

Figure 116 . Silver taler of Eichstatt (1781). View of city surmounted by Eye of Providence.

Figure 117 (below) Scheme of universe from *Janitor Pansophus* of *Musaeum Hermeticum* (1678 edition). Triangle is central and surrounded by symbols of Trinity.

Figure 118. Alchemical plate from *Janitor Pansophus*. First triangle on left contains tetragram. Alpha and Omega are inscribed below.

Figure 119. Plate from *Janitor Pansophus*. Prominent central triangle encloses tetragram, which is surrounded by words "Pater Filius et Spiritus Sanctus." Three sides of triangle are labeled TRI—UNI—TAS.

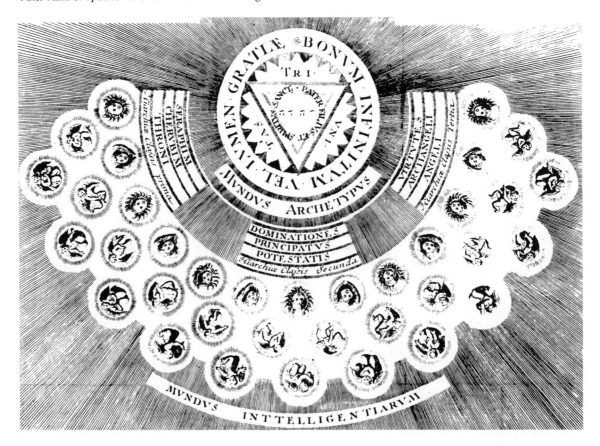

Quæ sunt in superis, hæc inferioribus insunt :
Quod monstrat cælum, id terra frequenter habet.
Ignis Aqua et fluitans: duo sunt contraria: felix,
Talia si jungis: sit tibi scire satis.
D.M.a C.B.P.L.C.

Figure 120. Frontispiece of *Musaeum Hermeticum* (1625 edition).
Three figures above cave carry triangular symbols for fire and
water and the combined symbol for fire plus water.

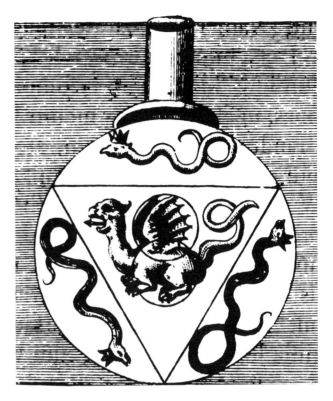

Figure 121. Figure from *Tripus Aureus* (1618), reprinted in
Chymisches Lustgärtlein (1624). Summary of preparation of
philosopher's stone. Three crowned serpents symbolize three
fundamental substances sulfur, mercury, and salt.

Figure 122. Figure from *Tripus Aureus*, reprinted in *Chymisches
Lustgärtlein*. Latin inscriptions along legs of triangle are mystical.
Symbols for gold (upper left), silver (upper right), and mercury
(bottom) are standard alchemical symbols. Hebrew lettering
makes nonsense words. This is "Tenth Key of Basil Valentine."

the first of these the triangle is central to the entire
scheme of universal symbolism. In the second the triangle inscribed in the circle represents God before the
act of creation. In the third the inscription surrounding
the triangle leaves no doubt regarding its trinitarian
implications. Lest these be thought to be the fixation of
a single writer, consider the following alchemical alle-
gorical pictures (Figs. 120-23). The first is the frontispiece of the entire collection in the 1625 edition of the
Musaeum Hermeticum. The figures above the cave
carry the triangular symbol for fire, the combined
symbol for fire plus water, and the symbol for water.
In Figure 121 the three crowned serpents around the
triangle represent three alchemical components
thought to be elemental sulfur, mercury, and salt. The
next two figures were originally from the *Tripus
Aureus* of Michael Meier (1618). In the first, the corners of the triangle bear the symbols for gold, silver,
and mercury. The surrounding Latin inscriptions are
mystical and the Hebrew is nonsense. In the last the
triangular symbol for water is central to the four
seasons.[5]

Figure 123. Another alchemical diagram centering in triangle. From *Tripus Aureus*, reprinted in *Chymisches Lustgärtlein*. This is "Seventh Key of Basil Valentine."

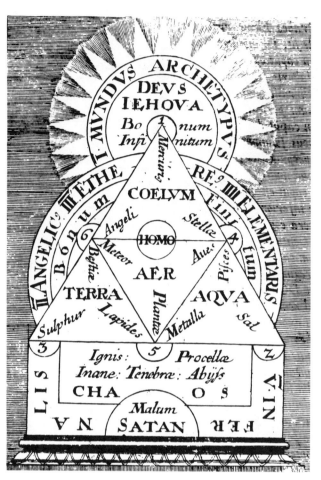

Figure 125. Crown of Nuremberg (1765). Within radiate triangle note thrice repeated Hebrew letter yod instead of the eye as in Fig. 116.

Figure 124. Symbolic cosmology built on triangles. From Roslin, *De Opere Dei Creationis* (1597), reprinted in Manget, *Bibliotheca Chemica Curiosa* (1702).

Figure 126. Triple yod in triangle as in "Auge Gottes" on numerous seventeenth- and eighteenth-century coins.

Figure 127. Title page of Heinrich Khunrath's *Amphitheatrum Sapientiae Aeternae* (1609). Pythagorean *tetraktys* arrangement of tetragram appears top center.

Figure 129. Diagram of tetragram forming *tetraktys* as in Figs. 127 and 128

Figure 128. Additional illustration from Khunrath showing same arrangement of *tetraktys* with further Cabalistic symbolism

Thus the triangle was a common alchemical symbol. Like many other alchemical symbols, it did not always mean the same thing, but in the later years of the seventeenth century it took on divine and trinitarian significance. However, even earlier one finds a symbolic cosmology built on triangles in Röslin's *De Opere Dei Creationis* (1597) (Fig. 124).

A very special case of divine triangle symbolism is found in some coins where instead of the eye in triangle one finds the Hebrew letter yod thrice repeated (Fig. 125). An enlarged view of this triangle appears in Figure 126. The key to the symbol lies in the work of the mystic Heinrich Khunrath, who published his *Amphitheatrum Sapientiae Aeternae* at Hannover in 1609.[6] Khunrath was influenced by the Jewish medieval mystics, the Cabalists. Their central text was the *Zohar*, a book of multiple and mysterious origins, which appeared first in thirteenth-century Spain. The wave of European mysticism of the seventeenth century swept up Cabala along with alchemy and astrology, and Khunrath, who appeared to know Hebrew, was one of its exponents. The key to the coin of Figure 125 appears on the title page of Khunrath's *Amphitheatrum* (Fig. 127) and on one interior plate as well (Fig. 128). At the apex of each of the two pages is a triangle containing Hebrew lettering reproduced in Figure 129. The lowest line of these letters is the Hebrew

Figure 130. Diagram of *tetraktys*

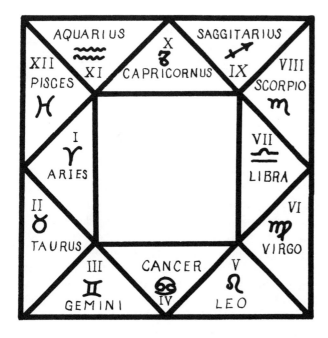

Figure 132. Standard astrological diagram composed of triangles

Figure 131 (right). Triple yod and tau cross on page labeled "Gott. Deus" from Comenius, *Orbis Pictus* (1679)

name of God. Often transliterated Yahweh, it is known as the tetragram. Above it in the diagram are the first three letters of the four (reading from right to left, of course); above it the first two; and at the apex of the triangle the initial letter only, the yod.

This might be considered a simple whimsy on the part of Khunrath if one did not know that the arrangement was adapted by the Cabalists from an even more ancient source. It is identical with the arrangement called the *tetraktys* of Pythagoras. The Pythagoreans were fascinated by the mathematical relationship $1+2+3+4=10$, and they expressed it using pebbles as in Figure 130. They considered this the fundamental arithmetical relation from which the rest of arithmetic was derived. It was so central to the Pythagorean brotherhood that novices took their oath of initiation on it.[7] The *tetraktys* was also the basis of the concept of "triangular numbers." Three, or six, or ten, or fifteen pebbles could be arranged similarly in a triangle and shared those special properties. Thus the triple yod in our coin of Figure 125 is at once a trinitarian symbol, a triangular number of Pythagoras, and an abbreviation for the full Cabalistic version of the *tetraktys* in the Khunrath engraving.

A variation on this theme, from the late alchemical work the *Orbis Pictus* of Comenius, is seen in Figure 131. Here the triple yod is accompanied by the tau cross and the plate is labeled "Gott. Deus."[8]

Other less specific obsessions with the triangle extend from Plato through astrology to the same baroque period that concerns us. When Plato devised the shapes of the atoms of the four elements—fire, water, earth, and air—in the *Timaeus*, he constructed four solids out of triangles to do so. Of the resulting solids

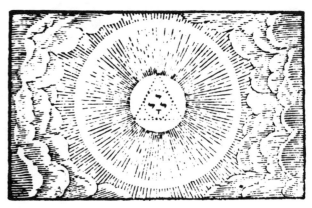

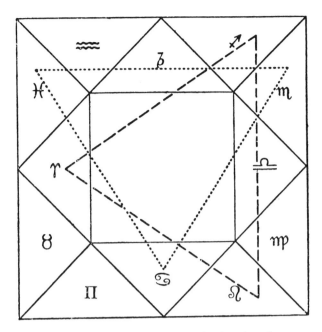

Figure 133. Larger fiery and watery triangles, based on diagram of Fig. 132

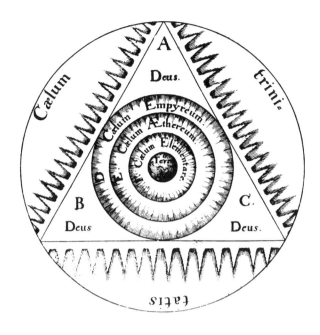

Figure 134. Rosicrucian triangular cosmic diagram. From Robert Fludd, *De Macrocosmi Principiis* (1617).

—the tetrahedron, the octahedron, the cube, and the icosahedron—all but one have triangular faces.[9]

This Platonic fascination with the triangle made its way into astrology. The customary horoscope displays the twelve zodiacal signs as a series of triangular subdivisions of a square (Fig. 132). Each triangle is devoted to a sign of the zodiac and is called a "house." The position of each of seven visible heavenly bodies (Sun, Moon, Mercury, Venus, Mars, Jupiter, Saturn) in the "houses" of the zodiac at the moment of birth of a prominent person was the basis for casting a horoscope for that person which foretold his future even to the hour of his death. To give the weight of classical physics to their activities astrologers grouped the "houses" into four groups of three each. These groups formed larger triangles and were called fiery (Aries, Leo, Sagittarius), watery (Cancer, Scorpio, Pisces), earthy (Taurus, Virgo, Capricornus) and aerial (Gemini, Libra, Aquarius) respectively. Figure 133 shows two of the large triangles. Thus the Platonic elements complete with triangles made their way into astrology.

Let it be remembered that during this period of the seventeenth century when all of the medieval mystical symbolism we have just been discussing was finally appearing in print, an entirely different set of events was under way. The foundations of modern science

were being laid. Galileo's *Dialogue on the Two Chief Systems of the World* appeared in 1632. Descartes's *Discourse on Method* was printed in 1637, and Newton's *Principia Mathematica* was dated 1687. However, it was to be another century before the intellectual and social effects of these efforts were to be felt. In the meantime our mystical triangle was carried through the first half of the seventeenth century and beyond by an underground secret society—the Rosicrucians. The dynamic of the society appeared to be philosophical, but mystery and pretension to antiquity were as characteristic of it as of the later phenomenon of Freemasonry. The sect was based on a series of anonymous revelatory books: the *Fama Fraternitatis* (1614 or 1615), the *Confessio Fraternitatis* (1615), and the *Chimische Hochzeit* (1616). All three are heavily loaded with alchemical symbolism to heighten the mystery. A major participant in the movement was the Englishman Robert Fludd, whose *De Macrocosmi Principiis* (1617) is a good example of Rosicrucian symbolism. Figure 134, showing a trinitarian triangle surrounding the universe is taken from Fludd. Rosicrucian brotherhoods perpetuated this symbolism through the seventeenth century.[10]

The origins of the Masonic movement are somewhat different from those of Rosicrucianism. By the

Figure 135. Triangular amulets
(Cyprus). From Ohnefalsch-
Richter, *Griechische Sitten und
Gebräuche auf Cypern*.

Figure 136. Beaded triangular amulet
of Bedouin origin (State of Israel)

Die Vorsehung
Gottes.

Providentia
Dei.

Figure 137. All-seeing eye (triangle omitted), labeled "Providentia Dei." From Comenius, *Orbis Pictus* (1679).

beginning of the eighteenth century the enlightenment of the new science, the rise of the landed gentry, and the leveling forces of early technology were beginning a ground swell in Europe which was to culminate in the great wave of revolution at the end of the century. However, that ground swell of the early years needed some shelter in secrecy. This was the origin of Freemasonry. In order to give dignity to a secret society its origins were placed in antiquity, but among members of a craft guild. There were, indeed, guilds of master masons during the great building period of the Middle Ages, but by 1700 these had long been quiescent. To add mystery a secret ritual was devised of bits and pieces. Some of these bits and pieces were Rosicrucian, harking back to the Cabala and alchemy. Indeed certain Masonic lodges fused with Rosicrucian brotherhoods. From the time in 1717 that four Masonic lodges met at the Goose and Gridiron Ale House in London and formed the Grand Lodge, the movement was under way. In its momentum it carried along our triangle symbol—found in any Masonic dictionary under the heading of "all-seeing eye" to its meeting with the committee on the great seal on that momentous July 4.

The triangle as an amulet can be documented in primitive societies but, of course, there is no way to get at the idea underlying this particular usage. Ohne-

falsch-Richter depicts the triangular amulet-pendant worn by Greek Cypriot peasant women in the early years of this century (Fig. 135) and shows the parallelism with amuletic pendants on figurines excavated on the island in the ancient sanctuaries of Apollo and Aphrodite (Fig. 136).[11]

The beaded triangular amulet in Figure 136 is made by Bedouins in Israel and represents a traditional design. Just as it is obvious that the triangle has divine significance and somewhere in the seventeenth century resumed its trinitarian meaning as well, so it is evident that the eye is likewise a divine symbol. The Bible is ample evidence for the antiquity of the symbol, and numerous passages may be cited as substantiation of the Eye of God concept. Among these are Ps. 11:4 and 139:16; Job 34:21 and 36:7; 2 Chron. 16:9. The keynote is struck by Eccles. 34:19: "For the eyes of the Lord are upon those that love him, he is their mighty protection and a strong stay."

In Mylius's *Orbis Pictus* one finds illustration 149 (Fig. 137) labeled "Die Vorsehung Gottes. Providentia Dei," in which that divine eye is illustrated as protecting man from the snares of the devil.

If there be any remaining doubt that this is precisely the meaning of the symbol, recall that in something like 90 percent of the occurrences of the *Auge Gottes* on coinage, the coin is struck by a German city and the symbol of the *Auge Gottes* appears over a view of the city. The symbol says just what it appears to say—that the Eye of God is watching over the city benevolently to protect it. No other interpretation is possible. This is one of the anchor bolts of the Watchbird concept complex.

The enthusiasm with which the *Auge Gottes* was incorporated into baroque art is clear from the large number of extant examples of its use; an exhaustive survey would fill this volume many times over. Let Figure 138 suffice. It is a photograph of the 1766 ceiling painting by Jacopo Guarana in the "Little Chapel" of the ducal palace in Venice.

Perhaps an even stronger witness to the force of the message of the *Auge Gottes* is the story of the "Supper at Emmaus" by Jacopo Pontormo, now in the Uffizi Gallery in Florence. This painting was originally created at the outlying monastery of Certosa di Val d'Erma when the plague was raging in the city, in the years 1523–1524. When the painting was originally done there was no more than an aureole above the head of Jesus, the central figure. However, during some subsequent (and not datable) restoration, the

Figure 138. Eye of Providence in baroque ceiling fresco by Guarana (1766)

picture was "emended" and it appears today with the *Auge Gottes* above the head of Jesus.[12]

To my mind the supreme testimonial to the force of the underlying idea of the *Auge Gottes* lies in the existence in Vietnam of the religious cult of Cao Dai.

The most succinct account of the origin of the cult occurs in Buttinger's history of Vietnam. Buttinger describes Caodaism as an amalgam of traditional religions already present in Vietnam (Buddhism, Taoism, Confucianism, and a belief in spirits) with the foreign elements of Christianity, Western philosophy, and spiritualism. The founder of the cult was a visionary named Ngo Van Chieu who communed with spirits on his island in the Gulf of Siam. One of the spirits was named Cao Dai. After the initial revelations in 1919 Ngo Van Chieu moved to Saigon and gained acceptance in a wide circle of Vietnamese officials.

One of these officials, Le Van Trung, was responsible for spreading the movement among the people. In November 1926 in a series of sensational sessions Cao Dai revealed himself as the incarnation of both Buddha and Jesus. He chose Le Van Trung as supreme chief of Caodism, and Tay Ninh, a town northeast of Saigon, as its capital. By 1954 the new religion had become so popular that its adherents numbered a million and a half persons.[13]

The symbolism of Cao Dai is most impressive and may be seen to its best advantage at the largest temple, located at Tay Ninh. The central symbol of the cult is the triangle whose three sides symbolize Sun Yat Sen, the founder of the Chinese republic; Trang Trinh, a Vietnamese diviner; and Victor Hugo. The center of the triangle is the all-seeing Eye of God. The *Auge Gottes* lives!

One is entitled to speculate why the committee on the great seal did not use the word for our symbol which had been universal in Europe for a hundred years: "The Eye of God." It is at least conceivable that "The Eye of Providence" represents a compromise arrived at between the Deist philosophy of Franklin and Jefferson, which minimized interference with the laws of nature, and the religious orthodoxy of the majority of the colonists.

In any case, the Eye of Providence, whose history has never been recorded, has a history for all that. It stands in the pages of the classic philosophers, the astrologers, and the alchemists, and is their legacy to the United States of America.

9. Epilogue: Ars Brevis, Vita Longa Est

This inversion of the first aphorism of Hippocrates is not for the sake of perversity. Hippocrates was rightly impressed by the complexity and difficulty—so much more complex and difficult in our day—of the science of healing, compared to the brevity of a single human life. However, the matters we have been surveying in this volume deal not with a single life-span but with the collective experience of humankind.

It makes little difference for our purposes whether *homo erectus* appeared 400,000 or 500,000 years ago or whether *homo sapiens* appeared 40,000 or 100,000 years ago. Compared to the four or five millennia of what we choose to call civilization, these are very long times indeed. This is the justification for inverting Hippocrates.

Through all of this period life was circumscribed by the things a single man could do with his arms, legs, and fingers driven by a one-manpower engine, but these things must not be underestimated. Collectively, hunting and gathering groups could cover great distances, given enough time. Crude rafts could cross sizable bodies of water, and canoes made with stone-age tools must have braved the Pacific in prehistoric times. Thus we conclude with a statement made early in this book. It is too much to say how much of the material in the preceding chapters belongs to the collective human consciousness because the "days of misery and nights of fear" were common to all men. Or conversely, given the enormous time of prehistory, it is too much to say whether any or none of the universal phenomena we have described resulted from actual cross-cultural contact.

We cannot know the answer to this basic question and we shall probably never know. Nor, for the purposes of this book do we need that answer. Suffice it to say that there exists a widely disseminated, in some aspects curiously unified, body of ideas which lies deep within all of us who share the human condition. The portion of that body of ideas which lies close to my professional life is a never-ceasing source of fascination and wonder. I have chosen to call it the World's Eye.

APPENDIX A

Gorgon Coins of Antiquity: Mints and Chronology

* 1.	Parium, Mysia	7th c. B.C.
2.	Athens (controversial "Wappenmünzen")	600 B.C.
* 3.	Lesbos	550-440 B.C.
4.	Olbia, Sarmatia (north shore, Black Sea)	550 B.C.
5.	Chaeroneia, Boeotia (Greece)	550-480 B.C.
6.	Cyrene, Cyrenaica (Libya)	525-480 B.C.
* 7.	Cyzicus, Mysia	520-440 B.C.
8.	Corinth (Greece)	500-431 B.C.
9.	Neapolis, Macedonia	500-410 B.C.
*10.	Clazomenae, Ionia	500 B.C.
*11.	Methymnia, Lesbos	500-450 B.C.
12.	Soli, Cyprus	480 B.C.
*13.	Abydos, Troas	480-450 B.C.
14.	Motya, Sicily (under Carthaginian domination)	480-413 B.C.
15.	Leucas (Corinthian island colony west of Greece)	460-420 B.C.
*16.	Apollonia ad Rhyndacum, Mysia	450-330 B.C.
17.	Populonia (central Italy under Etruscans)	450-350 B.C.
*18.	Celenderis, Cilicia	450-400 B.C.
19.	Praesus, Crete	450-400 B.C.
20.	Corcyra (island west of northern Greece)	450-400 B.C.
21.	Cranii, Cephallenia (island west of Greece)	431-330 B.C.
22.	Tegea, Arcadia (Greece)	431 B.C.
23.	Camarina, Sicily	413-405 B.C.
*24.	Selge, Pisidia	400-333 B.C.
*25.	Nagidus, Cilicia	379-374 B.C.
26.	Sciathus (island off northeastern Greece)	ca. 350 B.C.
*27.	Syria (coins issued under Seleucus I)	312-280 B.C.
*28.	Cebren, Troas (later Antiochia)	before 310 B.C.
*29.	Soli, Cilicia	300-80 B.C.
*30.	Astypalaea, island of Cos	150 B.C.
31.	Seriphos (island southeast of Greece)	150 B.C.
*32.	Aradus, Phoenicia	111-110 B.C.
*33.	Iconium, Lycaonia	50 B.C.
34.	Rome (as Republic)	47 B.C.
*35.	Aegae, Cilicia (cf. 29)	A.D. 200 or later
36.	Alexandria, Egypt (under Roman rule)	A.D. 244-249

* Location in Asia Minor, now central and western Turkey with its fringe of islands in the Mediterranean.

APPENDIX B

World Distribution of the Thread-Cross

NOTE: Most of the locations listed in Appendix B were compiled from the sources cited in the notes to chapter 7, and from the following additional sources: W. v. Blandowski, *Australia in 142 Photographischen Abbildungen*; A. M. Hocart, *Bishop Museum Bulletin* (Honolulu) 62 (1929); E. G. Burrows, *Bishop Museum Bulletin* 145 (1937); O. Reche, "Der Kaiserin-Augusta-Fluss" in *Ergebnisse der Südsee-Expedition 1908-1910* (Hamburg: L. Friederichsen, 1913); and H. Smethlage, *Zeitschrift für Ethnologie* 62 (1930): 111-205. Museum collections—notably those of the British Museum (gift of Dr. Clement), the Y. Laurell Collection of the Stockholm Statens Etnografiska Museet, the Leiden Museum, and the Amsterdam Museum—and objects in my own collection provided additional locations.

ANCIENT
Zappalan, central coast of Peru (A.D. 1100-1400)
Ancon, central coast of Peru (A.D. 1100-1400)
Antioquia, Colombia

MODERN
Australia
   Upper Sherlock River, south of Fortescue River, Western Australia
   Adelaide, South Australia
   Musgrave Range, South Australia and Northern Territory
   Beagle Bay, Western Australia
   Carnarvon, Western Australia
   Boulia district, west Queensland
   Broome, Roebuck Bay, Western Australia
   Fowler's Bay and Port Lincoln, Great Bight, South Australia
   Kimberleys, Western Australia
   Sunday Island in King Sound, Western Australia
   South Australia (Wallaby tribe)
   South Australia (Diäri tribe)
Other Pacific Islands
   Prince of Wales Island, Torres Strait
   Mabuiag Island, Torres Strait
   Mer Island, Torres Strait

   Astrolabe Bay, northeast New Guinea
   Helmholz Point, Maclay Coast, and eastward, northern New Guinea
   Waima and Pakao districts, British New Guinea
   Port Moresby, New Guinea
   Hood Peninsula, east of Port Moresby
   Mawatta, near Torres Strait
   Ron Island in Geelvink Bay, Dutch New Guinea
   Sepik River, northeast New Guinea
   Lovely Islands, off New Britain
   Matupi, northern New Britain
   Duke of York Islands
   New Ireland
   Feni Islands, Bismarck Archipelago
   Muthuata, Fiji Islands
   Hawaii
   Pingelap, Caroline Islands
   Yap, Ponape, and Kusaie islands in Caroline Islands
   Nauru, Gilbert Islands
   Lau Islands, southeast of Fiji
   Tonga Islands
   Wallis Islands, northeast of Fiji
   Timor, Indonesia
   Sawu, Indonesia
   Sumatra, Indonesia
   Matana, Celebes, Indonesia
Asia
   Salan Village, Southeast Asia
   Waabong-Tong, upper Burma
   Chittagong Hills, Assam
   Assam (Naga tribes)
   Tibet
   Peking, China
   Thailand
   Upper Tonkin, Vietnam
   Darkhanbel, Inner Mongolia
South America
   Colombia
   Ecuador

Brazil (many tribes in northeast)
Guayana (Arawak tribe)
Upper Tapanahoni River, Surinam (Ojona tribe)
Gran Chaco, Paraguay
Bolivia (Choroti tribe)
North America
Vancouver, British Columbia, Canada
California, U.S. (Hupa tribe)
Arizona, New Mexico, U.S. (Hopi, Zuni tribes)
Arizona, U.S. (Yuma tribe)
Mexico (Huichol tribe)
Mexico (Tarahumara tribe)
Mexico (Cora tribe)
Mexico (Tepecano tribe)
Europe
Pongau (Salzburg), Austria
South Tirol, Austria

Bavaria, Germany
Frisia, The Netherlands
Holstein, Germany
Denmark
Värmland, Sweden
Aland Islands, Finland
Vormsi, Osel, and northern mainland, Estonia
Les Landes, France
Ireland
Africa
Hans E. Kaufmann reviews the literature on Africa in "Das Fadenkreuz in Afrika," *Paideuma* 13 (1967):76-95; he lists thirty-seven documented appearances of thread-crosses which extend from the Mediterranean through equatorial Africa as far south as Angola. The paper contains a map with sites marked.

Notes

1. *Introduction*

1. Albert M. Potts, "The Eyes Are the Windows of the Soul," *American Journal of Ophthalmology* 75 (1973): 1052.

2. Carl G. Jung, *The Archetypes and the Collective Unconscious*, trans. R. F. C. Hull, in *The Collected Works of C. G. Jung*, ed. Herbert Read et al., Bollingen Series no. 20 (New York: Pantheon Books, 1959), vol. 9, pt. 1.

3. George W. Harley, *Masks as Agents of Social Control in Northeast Liberia*, Papers of the Peabody Museum, vol. 32 (Cambridge, Mass.: Harvard University Press, 1950), p. 2; Franz Boas, *Primitive Art* (New York: Dover Publications, 1955).

4. Otto Reche, *Der Kaiserin-August-Fluss*, Ergebnisse der Südsee-Expedition 1908–1910, vol. 1, ed. G. Thilenius (Hamburg: L. Friederichsen & Co., 1913); Edna McGuire, *The Maoris of New Zealand* (New York, London: Macmillan, 1968).

5. M. E. L. Mallowan, "Excavations at Brak and Chagar Bazar," *Iraq* 9 (1947):198–210; "The Early History of the Middle East," in *Cambridge Ancient History*, ed. I. E. S. Edwards, C. J. Gadd, and N. G. L. Hammond, 3d ed. (Cambridge: At the University Press, 1971), vol. 1, pt. 2, p. 997; E. Douglas VanBuren, "Amulets, Symbols or Idols?" *Iraq* 12 (1950): 139–46.

6. O. G. S. Crawford, *The Eye Goddess* (New York: Macmillan, n.d.).

7. Anthony Mancini, *Minnie Santangelo and The Evil Eye* (New York: Coward, McCann and Geoghegan, 1977).

8. *The Evil Eye*, ed. Clarence Maloney (New York: Columbia University Press, 1976).

9. Sir W. M. Flinders Petrie, *Amulets* (1914; reprint ed., Warminster, Wiltshire, Eng.: Aris & Philips, 1972), p. 2.

10. Albert M. Potts, "Idea and Amulet—The Watchbird Concept Cluster," *American Journal of Ophthalmology* 66 (1968): 284–92.

2. *THE EVIL EYE*

1. Sir E. A. Wallis Budge, *Amulets and Superstitions* (London: Oxford, 1930); reprinted as *Amulets and Talismans* (Hyde Park, N.Y.: University Books, 1961), p. 4.

2. D. R. Hughes and D. R. Brothwell, "The Earliest Populations of Man in Europe, Western Asia, and Northern Africa," in *Cambridge Ancient History*, ed. I. E. S. Edwards, et al., 3d rev. ed. (Cambridge: Cambridge University Press, 1970), vol. 1, pt. 1., p. 165.

3. Budge, *Amulets*, p. 358.

4. Ibid., p. 361.

5. Siegfried Seligmann, *Die Zauberkraft des Auges und das Berufen* (Hamburg: L. Friederichsen, 1922).

6. Martin Delrio, *Disquisitionum magicarum libri sex* (Mainz: Johannem Albinum, 1603); Frederick T. Elworthy, *The Evil Eye* (London: John Murray, 1895 reprint ed., New York: Julian Press, 1958).

7. George Sarton, *A History of Science* (Cambridge: Harvard University Press, 1959).

8. Sir Thomas Browne, *Pseudodoxia Epidemica* (London: Dod, 1658), p. 152; Moritz Bermann, *Alt Wien* (Vienna: Bermann und Altmann, 1888).

9. Pliny, *Natural History* 7.17.

10. Ibid.; Kirby Flower Smith, "Pupula Duplex," in *Studies in Honor of Basil L. Gildersleeve* (Baltimore: Johns Hopkins University Press, 1902).

11. Karl Abraham, "Restrictions and Transformations of Psychoneurotics; with Remarks on Analogous Phenomena in Folk Psychology," Chapter 10 of *Selected Papers of Karl Abraham, M.D.* (London: Hogarth Press, 1949); Sigmund Freud, *The Psychoanalytic View of Psychogenic Disturbance of Vision* (1910) in *The Complete Psychological Works of Sigmund Freud*, vol. 11 (London: Hogarth Press, 1957), pp. 211–18.

12. Ferdinand L. P. Koch, "Patron Saints of the Eye," *American Journal of Ophthalmology* 28 (1945): 160–72.

13. Phyllis Greenacre, "The Eye Motif in Delusion and Fantasy," *American Journal of Psychiatry* 82 (1926):553–79.

14. Jakob Grimm and Wilhelm Grimm, *Kinder und Hausmärchen gesammelt durch die Brüder Grimm*, ed. Friederich von der Leyen (Jena: Diderichs, 1912), 2:19–25. (Story 82 this ed., 134 in original).

15. Seligmann, *Zauberkraft*; idem, *Der böse Blick und Verwandtes*, 2 vols. (Berlin: Hermann Barsdorf, 1910); idem, *Die magischen Heil- und Schutzmittel aus der unbelebten Natur, mit besonderer Berücksichtigung der Mittel gegen den bösen Blick* (Stuttgart: Strecker und Schroeder, 1927); Liselotte Hansmann and Lenz Kriss-Rettenbeck, *Amulett und Talisman* (Munich: Callwey, 1966).

16. Sir W. M. Flinders Petrie, *Amulets* (1914; reprint ed., Warminster, Wiltshire, Eng.: Aris and Philips, 1972); Elworthy, *Evil Eye*.

17. Seligmann, *Böse Blick*, vol. 2, p. 7, Fig. 77.

18. Sigmund Freud, *Introductory Lectures on Psychoanalysis*, in *The Standard Edition of the Complete Psychological Works of Sigmund Freud*, vol. 15, trans. J. Strachey (London: Hogarth Press, 1963), pp. 158 f.

19. Ibid., p. 164.

20. Ibid., pp. 155–56.

21. Ibid., p. 158.

22. Budge, *Amulets*, p. 172; Elworthy, *Evil Eye*, p. 241.

23. Elworthy, *Evil Eye*, p. 259.

24. Emma Lila Fundaburk and Mary Douglass Foreman, *Sun Circles and Human Hands* (Luverne, Ala.: Fundaburk, 1957); Claude B. Moore, "Certain Aboriginal Remains of the Black Warrior River," *Journal of the Academy of Natural Science of Philadelphia* 13 (1905): 125–44; Robert L. Rands, "Comparative Notes on the Hand-Eye and Related Motifs," *American Antiquity* 22 (1956–1957): 247–57.

25. Carl Schuster, *Joint-Marks: A Possible Index of Cultural Contact between America, Oceania, and the Far East*, Mededling No. 94 Afedling Culturele en Physische Anthropologie, No. 39 (Amsterdam: Koninklijk Instituut Voor De Tropen, 1951); Miguel Covarrubias, *The Eagle, the Jaguar and the Serpent: Indian Art of the Americas* (New York: Alfred A. Knopf, 1954); Carl G. Jung, *The Archetypes and the Collective Unconscious*, trans. R. F. C. Hull, in *The Collected Works of C. G. Jung*, ed. Herbert Read et al., Bollingen Series no. 20 (New York: Pantheon Books, 1959), vol. 9, pt. 1, p. 337; Helmut Hoffmann, *Die Religionen Tibets* (Freiburg and Munich: Karl Alber, 1956), Fig. 11.

26. Hansmann and Kriss-Rettenbeck, *Amulett und Talisman*, p. 192–93.

27. Elworthy, *Evil Eye*, p. 331.

28. Budge, *Amulets*, pp. 53 ff.

29. Ibid., pp. 182 ff.

30. *The Jewish Encyclopedia*, ed. Isidore Singer (London, New York: Funk and Wagnalls, 1905), s.v. Mezuzah.

3. *THE EYE OF HORUS AND OTHER EYE AMULETS*

1. Sir W. M. Flinders Petrie, *Amulets* (1914; reprint ed., Warminster, Wiltshire, Eng.: Aris and Philips, 1972).

2. Sir E. A. Wallis Budge, *The Literature of the Ancient Egyptians* (London: Dent and Sons, 1914).

3. P. Jeandelize, "L'oeil dans la magie de l'ancienne Egypte," *Annales d'oculistique* 189 (1956): 3–18.

4. Samuel A. B. Mercer, *Horus: Royal God of Egypt* (Grafton, Mass.: Society of Oriental Research, 1942).

5. John D. Comrie, "Medicine among the Assyrians and Egyptians in 1500 B.C.," *Edinburgh Medical Journal* 2 (1909): 101–29; E. A. Wallis Budge, *Liturgy of Funerary Offerings* (London: Kegan Paul, Trench, Trübner and Co., 1909); Sir John Gardner Wilkinson, *The Manners and Customs of the Ancient Egyptians* (London: John Murray, 1837).

6. Comrie, "Medicine."

7. W. M. Flinders Petrie, *Gerar* (London: University College and Bernard Quaritch British School of Archaeology in Egypt, 1928); C. Leonard Woolley, "North Syrian Cemetery of the Persian Period," *Annals of Archeology and Anthropology* 7 (1914–1919): 115–29; C. N. Johns, "Excavations at Atlit," *Quarterly of Department Antiquities in Palestine* 2 (1933): 41–104.

8. Henri Frankfort, *Cylinder Seals* (1939; reprint ed., New York: Dover Publications, 1964).

9. Gustavus Eisen, "The Characteristics of Eye Beads from the Earliest Times to the Present," *American Journal of Archeology* 20 (1916): 1–27; Tsoming N. Shiah, "Date of Certain Egyptian Stratified Eye-Beads of Glass," *American Journal of Archeology* 48 (1944): 269–73.

10. Francis Llewellyn Griffith, *The Antiquities of Tel El Yahûdîyeh and Miscellaneous Work in Lower Egypt during the Years 1887–1888*, Egypt Exploration Fund, Memoir no. 7 (London: Kegan Paul, Trench, Trübner and Co., 1890); W. M. Flinders Petrie, *Hyksos and Israelite Cities* (London: University College and Bernard Quaritch British School of Archeology in Egypt, 1906).

11. Achik, *Antiquités du Bosphore Cimmèrien*, vol. 3 of C. V. Daremberg and E. Saglio, *Dictionnaire des Antiquités Grecques et Romaines 1*, (Paris: Librairie Hachette et Cie, 1877), p. 257.

4. *THE EYE OF MEDUSA*

1. Jane E. Harrison, *Prolegomena to the Study of Greek Religion*, 3d ed. (Cambridge: Cambridge University Press, 1922), pp. 68–72, 163–97.

2. Albert M. Potts, "Idea and Amulet—The Watchbird Concept Cluster," *American Journal of Ophthalmology* 66 (1968): 284–92.

3. Ovid, *Metamorphoses* 4.604–803.

4. A. Furtwängler, "Die Gorgonen in der Kunst," in *Lexikon der Griechischen und Römischen Mythologie*, ed. Roscher, vol. 1, pt. 2 (Leipzig: Teubner, 1886–1890), pp. 1701–28; Thalia Phillies Howe, "The Origin and Function of the Gorgon-Head," *American Journal of Archeology* 58 (1954): 209–21.

5. Barclay V. Head, *A Guide to the Principal Coins of the Greeks* (London: British Museum, 1959), plate I, no. 3.

6. Lilian M. Wilson, "Contributions of Greek Art to the Medusa Myth," *American Journal of Archeology* 24 (1920):232–40; Ernst Buschor, *Medusa Rondanini* (Stuttgart: W.Kohlhammer Verlag, 1958).

7. Homer, *Iliad* 5.738 ff.; 8.348–49; 11.32 ff.; *Odyssey* 11.633 ff.

8. Janus Six, "Some Archaic Gorgons in the British Museum," *Journal of Hellenic Studies* 6 (1885): 275–86; R. Engelmann, "Harpyie," *Jahrbuch des kaiserlich deutschen archäologischen Instituts* (1887), 1:210–12; A. De Ridder, "Amphores béotiennes a reliefs," *Bulletin de Correspondence Hellénique* 22 (1898): 439–71, plates 4 and 5.

9. Roland Hampe, *Frühe Griechische Sagenbilder in Böotien* (Athens: Deutsches Archäologisches Institut, 1936), p. 63; Humfry G. Payne, *Necrocorinthia in the Archaic Period: A Study of Corinthian Art* (Oxford: Clarendon Press, 1931), p. 80.

10. E. Douglas Van Buren, *Clay Figurines of Babylonia and Assyria* (New Haven, Conn.: Yale University Press, 1931); F. Thureau-Dangin, "Humbaba," *Revue d'Assyriologie* 22 (1925): 23–30; D. E. McCown and R. C.

Haines; assisted by D. P. Hansen, *Nippur I: Temple of Eulil, Scribal Quarter and Surroundings* (Chicago: University of Chicago Press, 1967).

11. Sidney Smith, "The Face of Humbaba," *Annals of Archeology and Anthropology* 2 (1924): 107-14; idem, "The Face of Humbaba," *Journal of the Royal Asiatic Society* 22 (1926): 440-42.

12. W. H. Ward, *The Seal Cylinders of Western Asia* (Philadelphia: J. B. Lippincott Co., 1910), pp. 211-12; Clark Hopkins, "Assyrian Elements in the Perseus-Gorgon Story," *American Journal of Archaeology* 38 (1934): 341-58.

13. Carl W. Blegen et al., *Troy: General Introduction of the First and Second Settlement* (Princeton, N.J.: Princeton University Press, 1950), vol. 1, pt. 1; Carl W. Blegen, *Troy and the Trojans* (New York: Praeger, 1963).

14. Corrado Cafici et al., *Reallexikon der Vorgeschichte*, ed. Max Ebert, vol. 12 (Berlin: Walter de Gruyter & Co., 1929), p. 188.

15. T. J. Arne, "Painted Stone Age Pottery from the Province of Honan, China," *Paleontologia Sinica*, series D, vol. 1, fasc. 2, "Geological Survey China (Peking: n.p., 1925).

16. Junius Bouton Bird, *Art and Life in Old Peru: An Exhibition* (American Museum of Natural History, 1962), pp. 145-209.

17. Otto Reche, "Der Kaiserin-Augusta-Fluss," in *Ergebnisse der Südsee-Expedition 1908-1910*, vol. 1, ed. G. Thilenius (Hamburg: L. Friederichsen & Co., 1913); René Gardi and Alfred Bühler, *Sepik: Land der Sterbenden Geister* (Bern: Alfred Scherz Verlag, 1958).

18. Fred D. Ayres, "Rubbings from Chavin de Huántar, Peru," *American Antiquity* 27 (1961): 239-45.

19. Paul Cyril Muick, "Gorgoneia in Attic Vase Painting" (M.A. thesis, University of Chicago, 1955).

20. Auction Catalog 34, *Kunstwerke der Antike* (Basel: Münzen und Medaillen, 1967); *Art of the Ancient*, André Emmerich Gallery (New York, February through March, 1968).

5. BEHIND THE MASK

1. C. A. Valentine, *Masks and Men in a Melanesian Society* (Lawrence: University of Kansas Publications, 1961).

2. Wilhelm Wundt, *Völkerpsychologie*, vol. 3 (Leipzig: Verlag von Wilhelm Engelmann, 1908).

3. Franz Boas, *The Mind of Primitive Man* (New York: Macmillan, 1931).

4. George W. Harley, "Notes on the Poro in Liberia," *Peabody Museum of American Archaeology and Ethnology* 19, no. 2 (1949): 3-39; idem, "Masks as Agents of Social Control in Northeast Liberia," *Peabody Museum of American Archaeology and Ethnology* 32, no. 2 (1950):3-45.

5. Phillip H. Lewis, personal communication to the author.

6. Otto Reche, "Der Kaiserin-Augusta-Fluss" in *Ergeb-nisse der Südsee-Expedition 1908-1910: II. "Ethnographie: A. Melanesien*, vol. 1, ed. G. Thilenius (Hamburg: L. Friederichsen & Co., 1913).

7. Herodotus, *The Persian Wars*, ed. F. B. Godolphin, trans. G. Rawlinson (New York: Random House, 1942), book 4.

8. René Gardi and Alfred Bühler, *Sepik: Land der sterbenden Geister* (Bern: Alfred Scherz Verlag, 1958).

9. Reche, "Kaiserin-Augusta-Fluss"; Kathleen M. Kenyon, *Digging Up Jericho* (London: E. Benn, 1957).

10. Edna McGuire, *The Maoris of New Zealand* (New York, London: Macmillan, 1968).

11. Meinhard Schuster, "Die Töpfergottheit von Aibom," *Paideuma* 15 (1969):140-59.

6. THE EYES OF ARGUS

1. Hans Christian Andersen, *Eventyr og Historier* (Odense: Flensted, 1959), 1:7; Vergil, *Aeneid* 6. 417-20; Ovid, *Metamorphoses* 1. 625 ff.

2. Phyllis Ackerman, *Ritual Bronzes of Ancient China* (New York: Dryden Press, 1945); Herrlee Glessner Creel, "On the Origins of the Manufacture and Decoration of Bronze in the Shang Period," *Monumenta Serica* I (1935): 36-69, Fasc. 1; Rudolph Chelminski, "China Unveils a Breathtaking Show of its Archaeological Treasures," *Smithsonian* 4 (1973): 25-35.

3. René-Yvon Lefebvre d'Argencé, *Ancient Chinese Bronzes in the Avery Brundage Collection* (n.p.: Diablo Press, 1966).

4. Florence Waterbury, *Early Chinese Symbols and Literature: Vestiges and Speculations* (New York: E. Weyhe, 1942).

5. Creel, "Shang Period"; d'Argencé, *Avery Brundage Collection*; William Watson, *Ancient Chinese Bronzes* (London: Faber and Faber, 1962).

6. Max Loehr, *Ritual Vessels of Bronze Age China* (New York: Asia Society, 1968).

7. Robert B. Inverarity, *Art of the Northwest Coast Indians* (Berkeley: University of California Press, 1950); Polly Miller and Leon Gordon Miller, *Lost Heritage of Alaska* (Cleveland and New York: World, 1967).

8. Franz Boas, "The Decorative Art of the Indians of the North Pacific Coast of America," *Bulletin of the American Museum of Natural History* 9 (1897): 123-76; Franz Boas, *Primitive Art* (New York: Dover Publications, 1955); L. Shotridge, "War Helmets and Clan Hats of the Tlingit Indians," *Museum Journal* (University of Pennsylvania) 10 (1919): 43-48.

9. Bill Holm, *Northwest Coast Indian Art* (Seattle and London: University of Washington Press, 1965).

10. George T. Emmons and Franz Boas, "The Chilkat Blanket," *Memoirs of the American Museum of Natural History* 3 (1907): pt. 1, 329-400; John Reed Swanton, "The Haida of Queen Charlotte Islands," *Memoirs of the Amer-*

ican Museum of Natural History 5, pt. 1 (*Publications of the Jesup North Pacific Expedition* 5) (1905).

11. Leonhard Adam, *Primitive Art* (1940; reprint ed., London: Cassell, 1963).

12. Carl Schuster, "A Survival of the Eurasiatic Animal Style in Modern Alaskan Eskimo Art," in *Indian Tribes of Aboriginal America*, ed. Sol Tax (Chicago: University of Chicago Press, 1952); Carl Schuster, *Joint-Marks: A Possible Index of Cultural Contact between America, Oceania, and the Far East*, Afdeling Culturele en Physische Anthropologie 39 (Amsterdam: Koninklijk Instituut voor de Tropen, 1951); Waldemar Bogoras, "The Chukchee," *Memoirs of the American Museum of Natural History* 11 (*Publications of the Jesup North Pacific Expedition* 7) (1904–1909).

13. Creel, "Shang Period"; Leonhard Adam, "North-West American Indian Art and its Early Chinese Parallels," *Journal of Royal Anthropological Institute and Man* 36 no. 1 (1936): 8–11; Carl Hentze, *Frühchinesische Bronzen und Kultdarstellungen* (Antwerp: DeSikkel, 1937); Boas, *Primitive Art*.

14. Alan R. Sawyer, "Paracas and Nazca Iconography," in *Essays in Pre-Columbian Art and Archaeology*, ed. S. K. Lothrop, et al., (Cambridge: Harvard University Press, 1961), pp. 269–98; Alan R. Sawyer, "Ancient Peruvian Ceramics: The Nathan Cummings Collection," (New York: Metropolitan Museum of Art, 1966), pp. 140–41.

15. Henry B. Collins, "Composite Masks: Chinese and Eskimo," *Anthropologica* 13 (1971): 271–78.

7. *THE OJO DE DIOS*

1. Carl Lumholtz, "Symbolism of the Huichol Indians," in *Memoirs of the American Museum of Natural History*, vol. 3 (New York: Knickerbocker Press, 1900), pp. 154–60; Carl Lumholtz, *Unknown Mexico* (New York: Charles Scribner's Sons, 1902).

2. Peter T. Furst, "To Find Our Life: Peyote among the Huichol Indians of Mexico," in *Flesh of the Gods*, ed. Peter T. Furst (New York: Praeger, 1972); Barbara G. Meyerhoff, *Peyote Hunt* (Ithaca, N.Y.: Cornell University Press, 1974).

3. Robert Mowry Zingg, *The Report of the Mr. and Mrs. Henry Pfeiffer Expedition for Huichol Ethnography* (New York: Stechert Co., 1938).

4. Willie Foy, "Fadenstern und Fadenkreuz I," in *Ethnologica* 2 (1913): 67–109; Gerhard Lindblom, "Thread-Crosses (Fadenkreuze), Particularly in South America and Africa," *Ethnos* 5 (1940): 89–111.

5. Samuel Kirkland Lothrop and Joy Mahler, "A Chancay-Style Grave at Zapallan, Peru," *Papers of the Peabody Museum* 50 (1957): 2–25; Alfred Louis Kroeber, "Proto-Lima: A Middle Period Culture of Peru," *Fieldiana: Anthropology* 44, no. 1 (1954); Lumholtz, "Symbolism," p. 160; Johann Wilhelm Reiss and Alfons Stübel, *Das Todtenfeld von Ancon in Peru*, vol. 1 (Berlin: Asher & Co., 1883);

Charles Empson, *Observations and Correspondence . . . Relative to Various Ornaments of Gold, Idols, Sculptured Stones, Coins, Etc.* (Bath: C. Empson, 1838).

6. Carl W. Blegen et al., *Troy: General Introduction of the First and Second Settlement* (Princeton, N.J.: Princeton University Press, 1950), vol. 1, pt. 1; Carl W. Blegen, *Troy and the Trojans* (New York: Praeger, 1963); L. Bernabo Brea, *Sicily before the Greeks*, rev. ed. (London: Thames and Hudson, 1966); Corrado Cafici, "Sizilien: Jüngere Perioden, I. Neolithikum," in *Reallexikon der Vorgeschichte*, ed. M. Ebert (Berlin, Walter de Gruyter & Co., 1928), 12:188–207; Hans Henning von der Osten, *Ancient Oriental Seals in the Collection of Mr. Edward T. Newell* (Chicago: University of Chicago Press, 1934).

7. Emil Riebeck, *The Chittagong Hill Tribes: Results of a Journey Made in the Year 1882*, trans. A. H. Keane (London: Asher & Co., 1885).

8. Hans Eberhard Kauffmann, "Das Fadenkreuz in Afrika," *Paideuma* 13 (1967): 76–95; Foy, "Fadenstern und Fadenkreuz I"; Lindblom, "Thread-Crosses."

9. Ernst Rackow and Werner Caskel, "Das Beduinenzelt," *Baessler-Archiv* 21–22 (1938–39): 151–84.

10. Elizabeth Andrews, "Rush and Straw Crosses: Ancient Emblems of Sun Worship," *Man* 22 (1954): 49–52.

11. Nils Edvard Hammarstedt, "Julrönn," *Nordiska Museet Fataburen*, 1919, pp. 139–42.

12. Hans Eberhard Kauffmann, "Das Fadenkreuz, sein Zweck und seine Bedeutung," *Ethnologica*, NF 2 (1960): 36–39.

13. Helmut Hoffmann, "Quellen zur Geschichte der tibetischen Bon-Religion," *Akademie der Wissenschaften und der Literatur*, in Mainz, no. 4 (1950): 125–44.

14. Ferdinand D. Lessing, *Yung-ho-kung: An Iconography of the Lamaist Cathedral in Peking*, Sino-Swedish Expedition Publication 18 (Stockholm, 1942); René de Nebesky-Wojkowitz and Geoffrey Gorer, "The Use of the Thread-Cross in Lepcha Lamaist Ceremonies," *Eastern Anthropologist* 3-4 (1949-51): 65-87; René von Nebesky-Wojkowitz, *Oracles and Demons of Tibet* (The Hague: Mouton & Co., 1956); Stephan Beyer, *The Cult of Tara* (Los Angeles: University of California Press, 1973).

15. Beyer, *Cult of Tara*; Lessing, "Yung-ho-kung"; Nebesky-Wojkowitz, *Oracles and Demons*.

16. Helmut Hoffmann, *Die Religionen Tibets* (Freiburg, Munich: Karl Alber, 1956).

8. *THE EYE OF PROVIDENCE*

1. Gaillard Hunt, *The History of the Seal of the United States* (Washington, D.C.: U.S. Department of State, 1909).

2. Aurelius Augustinus, "Contra Faustum XX, 6," in *Corpus Scriptorum Ecclesiasticorum Latinorum* (Prague & Leipzig: Tempsky & Freytag, 1891).

3. Gerard Van Loon, *Medallic Illustrations of the History of Great Britain and Ireland to the Death of George II*

(London: British Museum, Department of Coins and Medals, 1911), 2: 483, plate 43.

4. Carl G. Jung, *Psychologie und Alchemie, Psychologische Abhandlungen*, Carl G. Jung, ed. (Zürich: Rascher-Verlag, 1944), vol. 5; Evan Mauer, personal communication, 1974.

5. "Janitor Pansophus," in *Musaeum Hermeticum*, Johann Daniel Mylius, ed. (Frankfurt: L. Jennis, 1625, 1678).

6. Heinrich Khunrath, *Amphitheatrum Sapientiae Aeternae* (Hanover, 1609).

7. James A. Philip, *Pythagoras and Early Pythagoreanism* (Toronto: University of Toronto Press, 1966); Nichomachus of Gerasa, *Introduction to Arithmetic*, trans. Martin Luther D'Ooge (New York: Macmillan, 1926).

8. Johann Amos Comenius, *Orbis Sensualium Pictus Quadrilinguis* (Nuremberg, 1679).

9. Paul Friedländer, "Structure and Destruction of the Atom according to Plato's *Timaeus*," in *Philosophy* 16, no. 11 (1949): 225–48.

10. Arthur Edward Waite, *The Brotherhood of the Rosy Cross* (London: W. Rider & Son, 1924).

11. Magda H. Ohnefalsch-Richter, *Griechische Sitten und Gebräuche auf Cypern* (Berlin: Dietrich Reimer, Ernst Vohsen, 1913).

12. Sydney Joseph Freedberg, *Painting in Italy, 1500 to 1600*, Pelican History of Art (Baltimore, Md.: Penguin Books, 1970).

13. Joseph Buttinger, *Vietnam: A Political History* (New York: Praeger, 1968).

Index